DARK PSYCHOLOGY

Learn How to Analyze & Read People Using Body Language Analysis

(Boosting Your Emotional Intelligence and Building Your Skills in Nlp)

Sandra Brown

Published by Sharon Lohan

© **Sandra Brown**

All Rights Reserved

Dark Psychology: Learn How to Analyze & Read People Using Body Language Analysis (Boosting Your Emotional Intelligence and Building Your Skills in Nlp)

ISBN 978-1-990334-56-6

All rights reserved. No part of this guide may be reproduced in any form without permission in writing from the publisher except in the case of brief quotations embodied in critical articles or reviews.

Legal & Disclaimer
The information contained in this book is not designed to replace or take the place of any form of medicine or professional medical advice. The information in this book has been provided for educational and entertainment purposes only.

The information contained in this book has been compiled from sources deemed reliable, and it is accurate to the best of the Author's knowledge; however, the Author cannot guarantee its accuracy and validity and cannot be held liable for any errors or omissions. Changes are periodically made to this book. You must consult your doctor or get professional medical advice before using any of the suggested remedies, techniques, or information in this book.

Upon using the information contained in this book, you agree to hold harmless the Author from and against any damages, costs, and expenses, including any legal fees potentially resulting from the application of any of the information provided by this guide. This disclaimer applies to any damages or injury caused by the use and application, whether directly or indirectly, of any advice or information presented, whether for breach of contract, tort, negligence, personal injury, criminal intent, or under any other cause of action.

You agree to accept all risks of using the information presented inside this book. You need to consult a professional medical practitioner in order to ensure you are both able and healthy enough to participate in this program.

Table of Contents

INTRODUCTION 1

CHAPTER 1: WHAT IS AND WHAT IS NOT DARK PSYCHOLOGY 5

CHAPTER 2: THE SECRET TECHNIQUES OF DARK PSYCHOLOGY 14

CHAPTER 3: DARK PERSONALITY AND DARK TRIAD - MACHIAVELLIANISM, NARCISSISM, PSYCHOPATHY 21

CHAPTER 4: MIND CONTROL AND ETHICS 34

CHAPTER 5: MIND CONTROL TECHNIQUES 51

CHAPTER 6: HOW TO USE NLP TO MANAGE EMOTIONS .. 61

CHAPTER 7: BEHAVIORAL TRAITS AND CHARACTER QUALITY OF THE MANIPULATORS 84

CHAPTER 8: HOW TO MANIPULATE 95

CHAPTER 9: DARK PERSUASION METHODS 103

CHAPTER 10: A QUICK INTRO ON BRAINWASHING 120

CHAPTER 11: CONSPIRACY THEORIES 152

CHAPTER 12: HYPNOSIS- FACTS, FICTION, AND THE PSYCHOLOGY THAT POWERS IT 159

CHAPTER 13: HOW DARK PSYCHOLOGY IS USED IN RELATIONSHIPS 171

CHAPTER 14: FACTORS THAT MAKE YOU VULNERABLE TO MANIPULATION 181

CHAPTER 15: HOSTILE MIND TAKEOVER 188

CONCLUSION 201

Introduction

Dark psychology is defined as the science and art of mind control and manipulation.

All of humanity has this potential to victimize other humans and living creatures. While many restrict or sublimate this trend, some act on these impulses.

Dark Psychology seeks to understand those thoughts, feelings, and perceptions that lead to human predatory behavior. Dark Psychology assumes that this production is intentional and has a rational and goal-oriented motivation 99.99% of the time. The remaining 0.01%, under Dark Psychology, is the brutal victimization of others without intentionally or reasonably defined by evolutionary science or religious dogma.

The first part of this guide will spend some time looking at some of the different aspects of dark psychology. We will explore what it is, who is more likely to use dark psychology as we all have some of this darkness and manipulation within us, and more. We will end this section with a look at some of the best techniques that can be used when it comes to dark psychology and how they all work together.

From there, we'll move on to the idea of persuasion and how this technology will be so useful when it comes to dark psychology. We will talk about how persuasion and dark persuasion will be separated only by the intent of the person who uses them, by the elements of belief, by some of the techniques used with confidence and even by some of the ways to recognize when it is dark, knowledge is used against of you.

In the following two sections, we will spend some time exploring manipulation and empathy. We'll see what manipulation is and why it can work so well to help you achieve your goals and get what you need, regardless of who hinders you in the process.

Then there is a discussion about the use of empath and how it can benefit when it comes to dark psychology. Many times when we think we are empathy or empathy in general, we see it as a way in which someone is able better to see closer development and understanding between the two. But you can use your skills as an empath to influence others and get more out of what you want, and this final section will spend some time learning how to make it happen.

Dark psychology is something that has gained a bad reputation in our world, and most people are inclined to avoid using any of the techniques because of the laws and ethics found in most societies around the world. But as you will find in this guide, there are many different methods that you can use to make this dark psychology work best for you. When you are ready to bring out some of that darkness from within you to achieve your goals and dreams in life truly, be sure to check out this guide to learn how to get started!

Chapter 1: What Is And What Is Not Dark Psychology

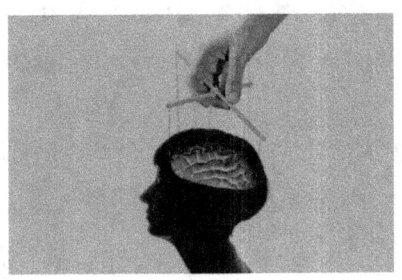

Dark psychology is the study of why some people are **horrible**. More specifically, though, dark psychology seeks to elucidate how and why some people prey on others. It assumes that everyone has dark urges sometimes—as humans, we simply can't help imagining being mean to someone or ways we could emotionally manipulate them into doing what we want. When we get angry, for example, we may exaggerate and say, "I just want to **kill** them" or "I'm so angry that I just want to hit them." Most of us would never really do those things, though—we suppress these sorts of impulses and don't act on them. We know that taking advantage of others and mistreating them is fundamentally wrong. Dark psychology seeks to understand those who are **not** like us—those who act on their worst urges towards others, who steal, cheat, lie, and continuously manipulate to get what they want or think they deserve.

This is in stark contrast to positive psychology, which studies which qualities and practices enable a person to live a happy, successful life. In general dark psychology, and its encompassed actions and behaviors can be traced back to the fundamental drive all humans have somewhere in their psyche to put their own goals and needs above others'. Forensic consultant and licensed psychologist Dr. Michael Nuccitelli did the pioneering work to develop this concept of dark psychology as a separate field. He sought to understand the thought processes that lead human beings to prey on others. In Dark Psychology, there is an assumption that while some predators commit atrocious acts for sex, money, or some other goal, others do terrible things without a purpose. They simply want to hurt someone or feel powerful just for the sake of it.

Before we go into further depth on dark psychology, there are some concepts you should keep in mind. The first one is dark continuum. Naturally, most callous, manipulative behavior exists somewhere on a spectrum. The dark continuum refers to the fact that these sorts of behaviors can range from being a slight nuisance to other people to causing harm and death. Where one's actions fit in along the dark continuum is called the dark factor. Everyone has a dark factor to some degree or another, but it is not the same. A person's dark factor is the result of their experiences, genetics, and personality. For example, someone may develop a more vital dark element if they grow up in an abusive household because they have seen despicable behavior normalized and learned that hurting others is acceptable. The dark singularity is the theoretical place in a person's mind that allows them to commit terrible acts without a purpose. The dark singularity is the place in someone's mind that wants to hurt others only for its own sake. As a dark factor, the dark singularity is on the dark continuum's rightmost end, which no one ever reaches. However, the most extreme psychopaths, such as murderers and rapists, are unconsciously always searching to reach this place. No one can get it, however, because all behavior is purposive to some degree or another. Hurting someone for no reason other than to feel powerful still means there is a purpose to the offensive action.

When you combine the dark continuum and the dark factor, you get the dark singularity. Factors outside a person's control, such a circumstance, and opportunity, either hinder or facilitate someone's ability to reach the dark singularity. The destructive person is always attempting to approach the dark singularity but never can. So, when you take the dark continuum, whose unclear factors are affected by outside circumstances, you can see how close someone comes to the dark singularity.

For a brief introduction to what dark psychology may look like in your own life, I'll provide a few examples of what dark psychology looks like in everyday instances. Have you ever met someone who showers you with affection and tells you you're perfect for them, despite not knowing each other very well? This type of person will shower you with compliments and gifts and **continuously** remind you of their undying commitment to you. Then they reveal their true selves—as soon as you disagree with this person or give them any reason to doubt your reciprocity, they will turn on you. They may call you selfish or become very angry and abusive towards you. This is called love bombing. It works because showering you with affection will make you more committed to the relationship and more likely to entangle yourself with this person, giving you no way to leave them. Once you are trapped, the abusive person can reveal their true self; their inner core is manipulative, possessive, and downright nasty.

The choice restriction is another common tactic you have probably experienced. The choice restriction is when a person may give you individual choices about a decision to distract you from the selection they do not want you to make. An example of choice restriction may be speaking favorably about two choices a person may have: the manipulator's more desired outcomes and ignoring or talking badly about the third option. Objectively speaking, all three options are equally valid in the situation. Still, the manipulator seeks a specific outcome, so he or she will distort information about each of the three to push their victim in the direction they want them to go.

Also, you've experienced covert emotional manipulation (CEM) or maybe even done it yourself. CEM is a tactic wherein the manipulator uses subtle cues and actions to manipulate someone. It may include the silent treatment or guilt-tripping. Essentially, CEM unconsciously leads the victim to doubt themselves or feel more reliant or indebted to the manipulator. Over time, the victim may continuously second guess themselves, have low self-esteem, or do anything they can to please the manipulator and not incur any more CEM tactics.

So, why is dark psychology-- the science of evil, meanness, cruelty, and callousness— worth studying and devoting a whole vocabulary too? By knowing more about the worst individuals, we can protect ourselves—while we may not be able to empathize with those who seek to hurt us, and we shouldn't understanding what their tactics may be. The signs of a manipulative or cruel person may help us avoid them.

From a more clinical standpoint, all humans have a lot to learn about ourselves from those among us who are most evil. Those with antisocial personality disorder (ASPD), known as psychopaths, can teach us quite a bit about responses to stressors and the reasons and mechanisms through which some people become impossibly cruel. ASPD can be thought of as consisting of two significant pieces; one piece is a personality lacking in remorse and empathy with little emotional depth, callousness, and a lack of care and regard for others. The other work of this personality disorder is antisocial behavior. Antisocial behaviors include patterns such as poor impulse control, inappropriate displays of anger, and irresponsibility. The core emotional and personality traits of ASPD seem to be highly heritable, which means that having a close relative, such as a parent, with these traits significantly increases the likelihood that you will have them. Higher levels of the personality traits associated with this disorder are relatively reliable predictors of the associated behaviors beforehand described.

Aside from these facts, there are a few others that may surprise you. For example, while the personality traits associated with ASPD may be highly heritable, the behaviors are not. In other words, having a cruel parent will not necessarily make you a nasty person. Instead of being a matter of genetics, the risk of engaging in antisocial behaviors seemed to be determined more by environmental factors a child may have been exposed to, such as trauma, poverty, or a delinquent group of friends. These risk factors, however, tend not to precede the antisocial personality traits a child may possess. In other words, personality traits determined by genes combined with an environment leading to antisocial behavior make a psychopath.

What does this tell us about ourselves? From antisocial personality disorder, we can understand that darkness and evil can consume anyone, depending on their surroundings and upbringing. While those who have been mistreated by a parent and develop this disorder don't have a choice, as adults, we may surround ourselves with those who bring out the worst in us, even if we will never develop a full-blown personality disorder.

Chapter 2: The Secret Techniques Of Dark Psychology

Manipulators, narcissists, and other adepts in dark psychology have their treasure trove of secrets that allow them to read people and bend them to their will. Narcissists are particularly skillful at reading others, poising them to seek romantic partners based on their perception that they can control them. Below is a list of some of the dark psychology secrets that can help you read people more skillfully.

Secret One

Be conscious of clues that suggest the other person is trying to establish rapport with you, such as mimicking your gestures and words.

This is really about paying attention. Most people do not notice the things that others do to try and establish a connection with them. In truth, the only people who usually notice this are those who have been manipulated before or the manipulators themselves. Although those who truly want to be our friend can indeed show signs of closeness, this tactic is often used by those whose goal is to manipulate or harm.

Secret Two

Others are trying to read you too, so be guarded in the information that you share.

You are not the only one out there trying to read the nonverbal and verbal cues of others. Other people are trying to read you too, potentially using that information against you. At the same time that you are reading others, you may want to be a little guarded yourself.

Secret Three

Be aware of when you are engaging in actions that seem not to benefit yourself.

This secret comes from the victims of narcissists. Although this book has generally approached the subject of reading people to influence them later potentially, it is also important to recognize signs that you are a potential target of someone else. Engaging in actions that benefit the other party frequently occurs in narcissistic relationships, even brief ones such as coworkers in an office, so pay attention to your actions in interactions and think about where they are coming from.

Secret Four

Instead of taking words at face value, always question what the motives of others are.

Although no one wants to suspect everyone they meet as being a liar and manipulator, the reality is that the world is in some respects a different place than it was fifty years ago. We do not live in communities where we share the same goals as those around us, and we knew everyone's name. Now, we have to be on guard for those who may wish to control us. Always think in the back of your head what the intentions of the other person are. This is important in verbal communication as well as nonverbal communication.

Secret Five

The use of vague or nonspecific language can be indicative of an attempt at mind control.

Be wary of when the person you are reading uses vague language. This can either be a sign that they are attempting to weasel themselves out of a lie, or it can be a clue that they are engaging in a mind-control tactic. As we have seen, suggestive words can be buried in otherwise innocuous or meaningless sentences, so be on the lookout for vague or confusing language.

Secret Six

Touching is a sign that someone wants to establish rapport with you or control you.

Touching and what it represents is an aspect of reading others that everyone should know. When someone is touching you, it always indicates something. A manipulator will touch you during a conversation because they have designs regarding you and need to establish rapport. But someone who likes you or who is your friend also may touch you. Use this body language cue in conjunction with others to get a sense of what is going on.

Secret Seven

Learning to read micro-expressions will improve your reading abilities considerably.

Microexpressions are facial expressions that last less than half a second. That means they appear on the face and leave very quickly. But if you learn to recognize these, you will gain an insight into others that very few have. Learn to notice when someone's expression seems to change very quickly. Pay special attention to the eyes.

Secret Eight

A sudden pause or looking away can be a sign that someone is lying.

A pause gives the other person to stall, giving them a chance to think of what to say. This can be a sign that the other person is lying. Think about it. When we are intoxicated, we speak honestly because we do not think about what we are saying beforehand. When someone is taking time to think about their words, it can often indicate deception.

Secret Nine

Use your intuition.

It is not always easy to use this particular tidbit of advice because intuition develops over time. If you are not used to analyzing others, you will likely lack the instinct about people. Let us face it; men often do not use their intuition when reading others because they tend to focus on verbal communication rather than nonverbal communication. Start to read the body language of others and develop a sense of what it means. Your judgments will be honed through a process of trial and error. Then, in the future, use your intuition to guide you.

Secret Ten

Learn the clues that indicate how someone thinks.

When we say how someone thinks, we mean how they process information. NLP manipulators learn what side of their target's brain is dominant and use eye movements to gain information about how the brain processes information. This is not easy, but it is a valuable skill that can be developed over time. Watch the eyes and learn to make a connection between eye movement and how the other person thinks.

Chapter 3: Dark Personality And Dark Triad - Machiavellianism, Narcissism, Psychopathy

Dark psychology is not a single, universally applicable medical diagnosis that can be applied across all cases of deviant personalities. There are, in fact, a wide variety of ways that dark psychology may manifest itself in someone's psychological and behavioral makeup. There is no absolute division of one deviant personality type from another, and many deviant personalities with prominent features of dark psychology may display elements of more than one manifestation of dark psychology.

This chapter will explore three types of dark psychology personalities.

It is important to remember that although the internet has spawned a huge growth in problems resulting from dark psychology, these traits have been part of human culture since ancient times. In fact, one of the dark psychology profiles we will explore in this chapter, Machiavellianism, takes its name from a medieval politician. Another, narcissism, takes its name from an ancient mythological character. Together, the three dark psychology profiles discussed in this chapter—psychopathy, Machiavellianism, and narcissism—make up what is known as "the Dark Triad."

Psychopathy

Psychopathy is defined as a mental disorder with several identifying characteristics that include antisocial behavior, amorality, an inability to develop empathy or to establish meaningful personal relationships, extreme egocentricity, and recidivism, with repeated violations resulting from an apparent inability to learn from the consequences of earlier transgressions. Antisocial behavior, in turn, is defined as behavior based upon a goal of violating formal and/or informal rules of social conduct through criminal activity or through acts of personal, private protest, or opposition, all of which is directed against other individuals or society in general.

Egocentricity is behavior is when the offending person sees himself or herself as the central focus of the world, or at least of all dominant social and political activity. Empathy is the ability to view and understand events, thoughts, emotions, and beliefs from the perspective of others, and is considered one of the most important psychological components for establishing successful, ongoing relationships.

Amorality is entirely different from immorality. An immoral act is an act which violates established moral codes. A person who is immoral can be confronted with his or her actions with the expectation that he or she will recognize that his or her actions are offensive form a moral, if not a legal, standpoint. Amorality, on the other hand, represents a psychology that does not recognize that any moral codes exist, or if they do, that they have no value in determining whether or not to act in one way or another.

Thus, someone displaying psychopathy may commit horrendous acts that cause tremendous psychological and physical trauma and not ever understand that what he or she has done is wrong.

Worse still, those who display signs of psychopathy usually worsen over time because they are unable to make the connection between the problems in their lives and in the lives of those in the world around them and their own harmful and destructive actions.

Machiavellianism

Strictly defined, Machiavellianism is the political philosophy of Niccolò Machiavelli, who lived from 1469 until 1527 in Italy. In contemporary society, Machiavellianism is a term used to describe the popular understanding of people who are perceived as displaying very high political or professional ambitions. In psychology, however, the Machiavellianism scale is used to measure the degree to which people with deviant personalities display manipulative behavior.

Machiavelli wrote The Prince, a political treatise in which he stated that sincerity, honesty, and other virtues were certainly admirable qualities, but that in politics, the capacity to engage in deceit, treachery, and other forms of criminal behavior were acceptable if there were no other means of achieving political aims to protect one's interests.

Popular misconceptions reduce this entire philosophy to the view that "the end justifies the means." To be fair, Machiavelli himself insisted that the more important part of this equation was ensuring that the end itself must first be justified.

Furthermore, it is better to achieve such ends using means devoid of treachery whenever possible because there is less risk to the interests of the actor.

Thus, seeking the most effective means of achieving a political end may not necessarily lead to the most treacherous. In addition, not all political ends that have been justified as worth pursuing must be pursued. In many cases, the mere threat that a certain course of action may be pursued may be enough to achieve that end. In some cases, the treachery may be as mild as making a credible threat to take action that is not really even intended.

In contemporary society, many people overlook the fact that Machiavellianism is part of the "Dark Triad" of dark psychology and tacitly approve of the deviant behavior of political and business leaders who are able to amass great power or wealth. However, as a psychological disorder, Machiavellianism is entirely different from a chosen path to political power.

The person displaying Machiavellian personality traits does not consider whether his or her actions are the most effective means to achieving his or her goals, whether there are alternatives that do not involve deceit or treachery, or even whether the ultimate result of his or her actions is worth achieving. The Machiavellian personality is not evidence of a strategic or calculating mind attempting to achieve a worthwhile objective in a contentious environment. Instead, it is always on, whether the situation calls for a cold, calculating, and manipulative approach or not.

For example, we have all called in sick to work when we really just wanted a day off. But for most of us, such conduct is not how we behave normally, and after such acts of dishonesty, many of us feel guilty. Those who display a high degree of Machiavellianism would not just lie when they want a day off; they see lying and dishonesty as the only way to conduct themselves in all situations, regardless of whether doing so results in any benefit.

What's more, because of the degree of social acceptance and tacit approval granted to Machiavellian personalities who successfully attain political power, their presence in society does not receive the kind of negative attention accorded to the other two members of the Dark Triad—psychopathy and narcissism.

Narcissism

The term "narcissism" originates from an ancient Greek myth about Narcissus, a young man who saw his reflection in a pool of water and fell in love with the image of himself. In clinical psychology, narcissism as an illness was introduced by Sigmund Freud and has continually been included in official diagnostic manuals as a description of a specific type of psychiatric personality disorder.

In psychology, narcissism is defined as a condition characterized by an exaggerated sense of importance, an excessive need for attention, a lack of empathy, and, as a result, dysfunctional relationships. Commonly, narcissists may outwardly display an extremely high level of confidence, but this façade usually hides a very fragile ego and a high degree of sensitivity to criticism. There is often a large gulf between a narcissist's highly favorable view of himself or herself, the resulting expectation that others should extend to him or her favors and special treatment, and the disappointment when the results are quite negative or otherwise different. These problems can affect all areas of the narcissist's life, including personal relationships, professional relationships, and financial matters.

As part of the Dark Triad, those who exhibit traits resulting from Narcissistic Personality Disorder (NPD) may engage in relationships characterized by a lack of empathy. For example, a narcissist may demand constant comments, attention, and admiration from his or her partner, but will often appear unable or unwilling to reciprocate by displaying concern or responding to the concerns, thoughts, and feelings of his or her partner.

Narcissists also display a sense of entitlement and expect excessive reward and recognition, but usually without ever having accomplished or achieved anything that would justify such feelings. There is also a tendency toward excessive criticism of those around him or her, combined with heightened sensitivity when even the slightest amount of criticism is directed at him or her.

Thus, while narcissism in popular culture is often used as a pejorative term and an insult aimed at people like actors, models, and other celebrities who display high degrees of self-love and satisfaction, NPD is actually a psychological term that is quite distinct from merely having high self-esteem.

The key to understanding this aspect of dark psychology is that the narcissist's image of himself or herself is often completely and entirely idealized, grandiose, and inflated and cannot be justified with any factual, meaningful accomplishments or capacities that may make such claims believable. As a result of this discord between expectation and reality, the demanding, manipulative, inconsiderate, self-centered, and arrogant behavior of the narcissist can cause problems not only for himself or herself, but for all of the people in his or her life.

The Dark Triad in Practice

The professional workplace has acknowledged the presence of people exhibiting Dark Triad characteristics. The following diagram illustrates that they are tolerated for their efficiency and their ability to get things done but contrasts that ability with the negative effects it has on their ability to form personal relationships:

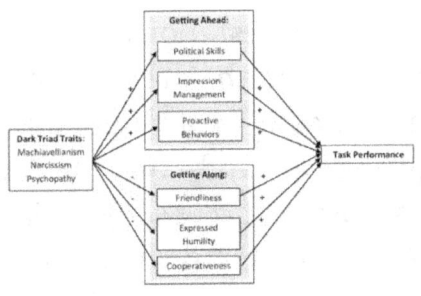

(McLarty, 2015)

The remainder of this book discusses a wide variety of people and situations in which you may find one, two, all three, or some combination of these Dark Triad personalities working in concert around you.

The clinical descriptions are easy enough to categorize, and in isolation, it can be fairly straightforward to separate one type of dark psychology from another. The real world is a lot messier. Many of us have grown accustomed to so-called "toxic relationships," whether they are relationships with our partners, our co-workers, our family members, our bosses, or our political and community leaders. In addition, manifestations of dark psychology are often far more mundane than the dramatic examples we see in major television and film productions about the romantic lives of serial killers and other criminals. The more we accept these relationships as normal, the more difficult it will be to identify them as problematic.

Remember that psychological, emotional, and social predators do not think of themselves as sick. Their lack of morality and empathy, and their adaption form a very early age to live according to rules and methods you may find horribly wrong, can make their presence intimidating. However, you should also remember that even when their amorality and lack of empathy may allow them to enjoy an unjust advantage in relationships, their mental capacities are the result of underdevelopment, not a higher evolutionary state.

Chapter 4: Mind Control And Ethics

Mind control is a loosely used term which can include many things, from little tricks employed by marketers and politicians, to serious brainwashing done by some religious cults or ideological organizations. All of them use psychology to manipulate others into doing what they want.

At the root of most mind-controlling behaviors is either personal gain or the desire to control. In individuals, these motives usually stem from self-esteem issues, the desire to gain or simply out of boredom.

Knowing you're being manipulated helps give a head start, so you can understand what's happening and then come up with an adequate plan to protect one's self. Being aware of a manipulator's game destroys any chance of it working. It's like not being impressed by a magician once you understand the mechanics behind the trick. But, if we're the ones doing the manipulation keeping our true intentions secret is paramount to having the desired success and not losing face.

There are different ways of manipulating, from very complex methods which need to be planned months or years in advance, to simpler techniques which can be applied right away, most manipulation cycles look something like this:

— Find someone's weaknesses (a desire to please, lack of assertiveness, fear of confrontation, naivety)

— Exploiting this weakness

— Benefiting

Ethical Use

We can make a case for the ethical use of Mind Control. In the realm of therapy for example. If someone gives a therapist consent to take over their mind to help them overcome some psychological issue such as anxiety or depression, this is considered positive use.

If we look at hypnosis, this could be deemed a form of mind control. It seems to be ethical because it has been consented by the patient and it offers the potential for positive change.

If you're strongly opposed to mind control even if it's used for 'ethical' reasons, then maybe you need to consider the many marketing strategies and advertising techniques we're subjected to on a daily basis to influence us into purchasing a particular product. Where do we draw the line?

It is too difficult to suggest all mind control is wrong and unethical. Is hypnosis unethical if it interferes with a person's free will and makes them change their way of thinking? Or if someone is about to commit suicide but another person uses advanced levels of mind control and psychological knowledge to talk them out of it, is that unethical? At the end of the day, is there much difference if someone physically makes someone do something through brute force or if someone influences another into action via mind control? If the end result is the same, then maybe there isn't much difference.

My own opinion on the matter is that if it is used for the greater good for the people involved then perhaps it should be acceptable.

Your own moral standards will decide how far you are prepared to go, or how low you will stoop to get something. The bottom line is, ethical persons use mind control in an ethical way, and unethical persons use it in unethical ways.

Some will claim everything is manipulative. However, it is more useful to consider influence on a range. One end of the spectrum is what's deemed the positive and respectful uses which consider people's rights. But on the opposite extreme we have more destructive forces, which tend to strip an individual of their independence, identity and the ability to think or act logically.

How useful is mind control?

Mind control is getting others to give us what we want when we want it. From the child who wants his parent to buy him a puppy or the boss who wants you to work overtime on a weekend without pay, mind control can work wonders if applied correctly.

Children are master manipulators. The child may at first beg with a soft pleading voice and eyes brimming with tears, but if that doesn't work, they resort to throwing a mini tantrum. Or, he may have figured out from experience which method works best when trying to get something from his father, and which one to use with his grandparents. As you can see, mind control is quite natural and something we learn early on in our development and perfect throughout life. We use persuasion techniques all the time but their success on larger scales depends on the power and shrewdness of the user.

Advanced mind control is a skill which can be honed through experience, knowledge and regular practice. If you're willing to learn you can develop a whole arsenal of methods to have at your disposal. This is important as it is unlikely one method will work every time or be effective with everyone.

Being a good persuader is easier if you're naturally good at reading people. But even if your mind-reading skills are not great, you should at least know what methods definitely won't work. For example, threatening your boss is rarely helpful. This approach is too overt and direct, so it can easily be thwarted by the other.

But when used subtly, mind control is incredibly influential. By simply choosing the right moment when asking for a pay raise, or knowing how to ask your father if you can use his car, these seemingly little factors may decide whether or not you get the outcome you desire.

Getting others to oblige to you regardless of how inconvenient the particular favor may be to them, can help you get more from life. However, there are some basic rules to follow.

3 things to keep in mind

— Know your place.

Be clear about what you are trying to achieve and from whom. Threatening your boss or someone you depend on, seldom works. On the contrary, it may even backfire. Instead be tactful.

— Choose the mind control method

Not every method works for everyone, or in all situations. By using the wrong method, you might miss out on getting what you want and make it even harder to achieve.

— Have a backup plan.

This is especially important if something big is at stake. Think things through, but anticipate things going wrong and be ready with an alternative approach or backup plan. If the first method doesn't work, be prepared to quickly and discreetly (in order not to lose face) try something else.

ISIS & Mind Control

In recent times, one of the more popular instances where mind control has been reported is by the Terrorist Organization Isis (Islamic State). From the UK alone, it is reported they have managed to recruit over 1,600 people (mostly young) to join their organization. What would make people leave the comfort of their western lives to go to war torn countries to fight or engage in a world of conflict?

The rise in numbers has been seen in what's deemed 'Online grooming'. Usually this goes on for a substantial amount of time before people blindly follow the wishes of such organizations. It has been said that the real reason westerns go and join this plight is actually more to do with the advanced manipulation techniques used as opposed to the actual cause.

Brain washing vs Mind control

Brain washing is more aggressive in nature. Sometimes people have to be taken by force and be subjected to brain washing tactics. Whereas mind control is much subtler. In the ISIS example, people are more likely to be 'seduced' by a recruiter - not sexually, but emotionally. The recruiter takes the role of someone a young person looks up to, sees as a friend, a parental figure or a mentor. This is an important dynamic to create for successful mind control.

This 'friendliness' creates an illusion of choice. This makes the indoctrination by-pass the conscious ego defenses and gets to work deeper within the psyche. The recruiters work by first finding similarities with the target, maybe they're also someone who moved from the west to come and join forces with ISIS - this creates a sense of empathy, understanding and a community based on shared beliefs.

Since most people are aware of such a terrorist organization, the group have to tread carefully as to not scare away any potential new recruits. It would likely start with a soft approach of the target. In the mind control world this would be termed the 'grooming seduction phase'. This is when flattery and compliments are used heavily, with the approach of 'How can we help you?'. This initial period builds the relationship and allows the manipulators to get their 'claws' into the target. Once they reach this point, they can then use threats to prevent you from leaving such as death threats, threats on the targets family and loved ones.

In the case of ISIS, most of the young people who are recruited don't really know what they're getting themselves into. They are given just enough information which allows them to create a fantasy in their mind. They may be convinced into believing they'll become saviors of their religion or help make world peace. This belief of a heightened sense of importance can become a very powerful motive in controlling people. Its only after joining such an organization do the recruits really begin to realize that it isn't what they expected. That in reality, they're probably not going to change the world but in fact have put their lives in grave danger.

For us people who are not involved, it is easy for us to point the finger and make judgements about those involved. But on closer inspection, we must try to realize there is something going on that would make someone join such an organization. It comes down to the use of social psychology and using it to influence people's motivation, interest and curiosity. In fact, most of the people recruited are likely to be good people. People who want to make a positive difference in the world, or want to improve themselves - by playing on these tendencies the target can eventually be manipulated into a new way of thinking.

Indoctrination Tactics

A popular model used in cults and extremist groups such as ISIS is called the four-part model. This points to the fact that most people fall into one of four categories - feelers, thinkers, believers or doers. The manipulator will start by analyzing the target to see which of these groups they fall into. For example, for feelers their motives are very emotionally driven and they want to feel part of a community or a social group. But for thinkers, they will have to be approached with more intellect and be engaged in more theoretical way. Whereas believers think this is their destiny and something which offers them deeper meaning to their life. Finally, doers are more concerned with saving lives, protecting people, fighting evil and preventing oppression of people. A skilled manipulator will be able to detect the specific personality type and find a way into influencing.

The information obtained about a person's personality can then be used to shape their character in the desired way. By controlling one of these four parts of a person, we can gradually begin to shift their identity to one which suits the cause or plight we're involved with. The new identity however, will be more obedient, have less independence or freedom of choice.

ISIS for example, may at this point give you a new name. People who have been indoctrinated in this way may even begin to believe they're above fellow human beings and are being led by some higher power such as God. This is a similar thing seen in religious cults all over the world.

Social Psychology

Most of us function under what is known as fundamental attribution of error - which is deemed to be one of the most important factors within Social Psychology. It basically means that, when we try to understand what others are doing, we have a certain error where we attribute most of the behavior on their personality and them as a person while under attributing the influence of social and environmental factors which also play a part in human programming and behavior. When we look at this closer, we tend to see that ISIS recruits are generally intelligent, good people from positive backgrounds. This points to the mind control and grooming which occurred to be quite substantial.

For mind control to work successfully, it requires the target to come back on their own accord, especially during the early stages of manipulation. By hooking them in, they can be led into believing they're coming back is their own choosing and the steps they're taking is mainly their choice.

Cults such as these will usually commit the target to keep things 'to themselves' and not to tell anyone. Also, to not change their behavior much because they're aware of how most families will react. Unfortunately, if we try to talk someone out of this, it can have the opposite effect and plunge them even deeper. Using authority and fear to combat such a problem seldom works. Instead it only works to convince the target they're on the right path. The reason why some of these recruits then go on to commit horrific crimes is because they have developed a new identity. They're not themselves anymore, from a new identity we can carry out acts and not really feel as though we were there. Especially when they're supported by others with the same thinking and beliefs.

The good news is that people who are indoctrinated, can be brought back to their true identity. Providing there is no mental health issues at play and they can be separated from the group or cult they were involved with. Of course, this doesn't occur overnight, and each case is subjective.

Mind control methods

Developing these skills requires an understanding of what you're doing. Which begins by knowing what you are trying to achieve (outcome) and who the target is.

1. Most common overt mind control methods

— Pleading (making promises, being nice, asking for a favor, crying)

— Making threats (threatening to harm others, threats to kill one's self, threatening to leave, firing you from your job, ruining your reputation, losing your title etc) if a request is rejected.

2. Religious cults and sects use mind control methods to recruit, indoctrinate and keep members, some of which include

— Mind-altering drugs

— Indoctrination with constant repetition and chanting

— Doublespeak (confidently using words in a way that don't mean what they seem to, in order to prevent coherent thinking)

— Detailed control (of who you speak to, what you listen to, who you socialize with)

— Enemy creation ideology (us vs them) - in an atmosphere of fear (including the use of ridicule and the creation of a siege mentality)

Chapter 5: Mind Control Techniques

It's interesting to see that manipulation has been around for a long time, and that is not a new or imaginary concept. Understanding what the art of persuasion is all about is vital, to help you to deal with it.

Here, we briefly look at the psychology of manipulation. This allows us to see where it might occur in our lives. It will also help you in identifying those who might attempt to manipulate you. It is not only about people who like to dominate. If we don't know it is happening to us, might be encouraged to act in ways that are incongruous to our normal personality and behavior. Learn how commerce can persuade customers into buying their goods and services. Recognizing such methods will help in dealing with the power of persuasion.

We like to believe that we are individuals who make sensible choices. In our journey of life, we do not always have full control, and we don't always realize this. As children, we are influenced by our parents and have little control over how we raised. Once in the education system, we are further manipulated. The teachers will tell us all about the social norms and what is expected of us in society. As adults, we are lured in by politicians trying to get their share of votes. Many are persuaded to vote for a party because of what they promise for the future, even if they don't necessarily believe in their policies. This gives such politicians power, and their decisions will affect our lives. Are we in full control of our lives, or are we merely influenced by those who know all the tricks of persuasion?

We will look at how to deal with various manipulative methods, even sometimes covert. First, you need to learn to recognize when you are being manipulated so you can counteract it.

Recognizing the Art of Manipulation

What then, in our everyday lives, do we need to be wary of?

Persuasive Language

The idiom that every picture tells a story is very true. Words can be so much more powerful as they inspire and encourage us, even to the point of manipulation. How many are the time you have been inspired by a good orator, who's daring speech motives you into action? The art of words can be so influential in coercing us to believe something, even when our eyes tell us differently. Communication is a powerful tool, especially when it comes to making people do things.

Advertisers and salespeople use language to convince their goods are just what we are looking for. Using words, such as:

Affordable; Easy to use; Safe; Enjoyable; Time Saving; Guaranteed to last.

Note how all these words make us believe they are confident in their products.

Politicians will use language, such as:

"We" - to encompass you in their world.

"Us" to make you feel a part of a team.

These are all communication tactics to make us feel included, so therefore important.

Bullies use language along with aggressive behavior, to achieve their own selfish goals.

Criminal predators, such as psychopaths, sociopaths and narcissists, are all people who learn the use of persuasive language. This is a means to get their way and gain control over another person.

Techniques Used in Mind Control

Present day mind control is both innovative and mental. Tests demonstrate that basically by uncovering the techniques for mind control, the impacts can be diminished or disposed of, at any rate for mind control publicizing and promulgation. Increasingly hard to counter are the physical interruptions, which the military-mechanical complex keeps on creating and enhance.

1. Education —it has consistently been an eventual tyrant's definitive dream to "teach" normally receptive youngsters, subsequently it has been a focal segment to Communist and Fascist oppressive regimes from the beginning of time. Nobody has been increasingly instrumental in uncovering the motivation of present day instruction than Charlotte Iserbyt — one can start investigation into this region by downloading a her book as a free PDF, The Deliberate Dumbing Down of America, revealing the job of Globalist establishments in forming a future planned to deliver servile automatons reigned over by a completely taught, mindful exclusive class.

2. Promotions and Propaganda – Edward Bernays has been referred to as the creator of the consumerist culture that was planned principally to focus on individuals' mental self-portrait (or scarcity in that department) to transform a need into a need. This was at first imagined for items, for example, cigarettes, for

instance. Nonetheless, Bernays additionally noted in his 1928 book, Propaganda, that "purposeful publicity is the official arm of the imperceptible government." This can be seen most unmistakably in the advanced police state and the developing native nark culture, enveloped with the pseudo-enthusiastic War on Terror. The expanding union of media has empowered the whole corporate structure to converge with government, which currently uses the idea of promulgation arrangement. Media; print, motion pictures, TV, and link news would now be able to work flawlessly to incorporate a general message which appears to have the ring of truth since it originates from such a significant number of sources, at the same time. When one moves toward becoming sensitive to recognizing the fundamental "message," one will see this engraving all over. What's more, this isn't even to specify subliminal informing.

3. Prescient Programming – Many still deny that prescient writing computer programs is genuine. Prescient programming has its causes in predominately elitist Hollywood, where the big screen can offer a major vision of where society is going. For a nitty gritty breakdown of explicit models, Vigilant Citizen is an incredible asset that will most likely make you take a gander at "amusement" in a unique light.

4. Sports, Politics, Religion – Some may resent seeing religion, or even legislative issues, put together with sports as a technique for mind control. The focal topic is the equivalent all through: isolate and prevail. The systems are very straightforward: impede common propensity of individuals to participate for their endurance, and train them to frame groups bowed on control and winning. Sports has consistently had a job as a key diversion that corrals innate propensities into a non-significant occasion, which in present day America has arrived at silly

extents where challenges will break out over a game VIP leaving their city. Yet, basic human issues, for example, freedom are chuckled away as immaterial.

5. Food, Water, and Air — Additives, poisons, and other nourishment harms modify mind science to make mildness and indifference. Fluoride in drinking water has been demonstrated to bring down IQ; Aspartame and MSG are excitotoxins which energize synapses until they kick the bucket; and simple access to the inexpensive food that contains these toxins by and large has made a populace that needs center and inspiration for a functioning way of life. The vast majority of the cutting edge world is flawlessly prepped for uninvolved responsiveness — and acknowledgment — of the authoritarian tip top.

6. Medications — we can equate this to any addictive substance, however the mission of mind controllers is to be certain you are dependent on something. One noteworthy arm of the cutting edge mind

control motivation is psychiatry, which expects to characterize all individuals by their issue, instead of their human potential. Today, it has been taken to considerably assist limits as a medicinal oppression has grabbed hold where about everybody has a type of confusion — especially the individuals who question authority. The utilization of nerve tranquilizes in the military has prompted record quantities of suicides. To top it all off, the cutting edge medication state currently has over 25% of U.S. youngsters on mind-desensitizing drugs.

7. Military testing — there is a long history associated to the military as the proving ground for mind control.

8. Electromagnetic range — an electromagnetic soup encompasses all of us, charged by present day gadgets of comfort which have been appeared to affect mind work directly. In an implicit affirmation of what is conceivable, one scientist has been working with a "divine being head protector" to instigate dreams

by adjusting the electromagnetic field of the mind. Our advanced soup has us latently washed by conceivably mind-changing waves. At the same time, a wide scope of potential outcomes, for example, phone towers is currently accessible to the eventual personality controller for more straightforward mediation.

Mind control is more common than most people think. It is not easy to detect because of its subtle nature. In many instances, it happens under what is perceived as normal circumstances like through education, religion, TV programs, advertisements and so much more. Cults and their leadership use mind control to influence their members and control whatever they do. It is not easy to detect mind control. However, when one realizes it, they can get out and start again.

Chapter 6: How To Use Nlp To Manage Emotions

In NLP, there is nothing of the sort as an un-creative individual, only an un-ingenious state. Having the option to deal with your state so you can stay creative even in the most testing circumstances is unmistakably something that is of gigantic worth any place you work, whatever you do and whoever you are!

Whatever task you need to play out, anything you desire the result to be, ask yourself - "what state would I like to be in to make this simple?"

On and when you would like to or need to change your state so as to assist you with performing at your ideal level then there are numerous approaches to do so utilizing NLP procedures.

To kick you off, here are 3 simple approaches to assist you with dealing with your passionate state:

1. Core interest

Change the photos you are making for yourself — what you are envisioning, yet how you are imagining it. Change the sounds you can hear, become progressively mindful and zone in for the most ideal picture. Ever seen what occurs in the event that you're feeling low or somewhat askew and, at that point you hear your preferred bit of inspiring music? Change the sounds and how you envision your final product to be.

2. Physiology

Change your body profoundly — Move, do whatever pushes various synthetic concoctions around your sensory system whether this could be accomplishing more exercise or just taking the stairs rather than the lift. Change your stance, stand tall, high and effective, not exclusively will you look certain, yet you'll feel increasingly sure. Consider changing your outward appearance as well and your breathing, even the littlest revises will assist you with dealing with your state.

3. Self-Talk

Change your inside exchange or self-talk. You can change the substance or the language of your mind jabber, so you become your very own hero. What about changing your inside pundit that discloses to you you're bad enough? Envision how amusing you may discover it if your internal pundit had the voice of Mickey Mouse or the Donkey from Shrek? Or then again move the area of the voices so it originates from your left huge toe!

All states are brought about by the association between your reasoning designs, your physiology and your neurochemicals. Changing any of these can impact your state.

The capacity to change your state and pick how you feel is one of the abilities for passionate opportunity and a cheerful life. Passionate opportunity doesn't mean failing to feel negative yet means you are increasingly mindful of negative states and can pick your reaction.

There are numerous manners by which individuals can build up the mindfulness to adequately deal with their states. This is only one of the numerous incredible procedures in NLP to assist you with performing at your best regardless of what is happening in your condition.

Improve enthusiastic insight with NLP

As we find out increasingly more about what makes individuals an accomplishment in business and particularly regarding administration, the widespread supposition is moving ceaselessly from the conventional traits of IQ and specialized capacity and towards enthusiastic insight. Passionate knowledge is currently observed as a "need to have" fixing in the make up of pioneers.

In contrast to our IQ, our enthusiastic knowledge is something that can be created and improved with preparing, and NLP Training does only that. Passionate insight is portrayed in its Wikipedia passage as "the capacity to recognize, evaluate, and control the feelings of oneself, of others, and of gatherings."

Enthusiastic Intelligence

Five components of our make-up that we could ascribe to passionate knowledge at work:

Mindfulness – How much do we comprehend about our very own temperaments, states, and feelings and how they sway on our conduct? Is it accurate to say that we are mindful of how our states of mind influence others? How effectively would you say you are ready to distinguish your very own qualities and shortcomings, qualities, needs and drives?

Self Regulation – How great would we say we are at intuition before we act? It is safe to say that we are ready to control our states of mind and motivations so as to maintain a strategic distance from our conduct having negative ramifications for us and for other people?

Inspiration – How solid is your longing to perseveringly seek after your objectives? How are your general vitality levels? Do you have an enthusiasm forever and for your work that is past cash and power?

Sympathy – How simple do we discover it to see someone else's perspective? What amount do we comprehend about the enthusiastic make-up of other individuals? How effectively do we adjust our very own conduct in the light of other individuals' passionate responses?

Social Skills – How effectively would you say you are ready to assemble affinity and discover shared opinion so as to adequately deal with your connections?

NLP tends to every last one of these zones and NLP Training is intended to work at the oblivious level to ensure that just as recognizing what you ought to do, you can exhibit skill in really doing it. It is just through preparing conduct into your sensory system that the conduct gets changeless and repeatable, and this is cultivated by working with the intuitive piece of your cerebrum.

NLP improves enthusiastic knowledge

How about we take a gander at how explicitly NLP can profit you as far as the five components referenced previously:

Self Awareness

In the NLP Practitioner course the underlying spotlight is on building up a comprehension of how your cerebrum works, how you develop your encounters and how your conduct is created. This empowers you to comprehend and perceive your mind-sets and states and see how you have achieved those dispositions and states.

A lot of NLP Submodalities work is tied in with empowering you to change your musings, feelings, different preferences by comprehension and controlling the better qualifications in the considerations that you procedure.

Self Regulation

NLP Anchoring empowers you to perceive and change your temperament in a moment. It additionally empowers you to set up triggers which will naturally deliver a positive feeling in you under explicit conditions. This can be helpful for circumstances where you ordinarily find that you carry on ineffectively previously.

In the Strategies part of the NLP Practitioner course we figure out how we have certain oblivious reasoning techniques that make up our practices. We figure out how to dismember these systems and change them to deliver better conduct in our quest for greatness.

Motivation

NLP is about results. It is tied in with choosing what you need, how you need to improve and finding a course to prevail with regards to arriving.

Utilizing NLP Submodalities and Timeline procedures you can make your objectives and targets convincing and direct your vitality towards accomplishing them.

Neurological Levels is a piece of the NLP Practitioner preparing and this reasoning empowers you to guarantee that you work, prepare and set targets for yourself as well as other people at a level that gives you reason and empowers you to accomplish any profound goals that you may have.

Empathy

Perceptual Positions is a fun practice that you learn in the NLP Practitioner course where you get to re-experience a past occasion where you have had a correspondence trouble with somebody, and you survey the circumstance from three heavenly attendants. You see the circumstance from your very own position, the situation of the other individual, and from the situation of a fly on the divider. This truly empowers you to start to make a superior compassion with others and to see things from alternate points of view.

In NLP, Sensory Acuity is tied in with perceiving minute changes in someone else that parts with how they are thinking, empowering you to perceive their states of mind, their temperament changes and their feelings.

The entire prospectus of NLP Master Practitioner preparing is equipped around empowering you to comprehend other individuals and what really matters to them. You figure out how to comprehend your own and different people groups esteems and characters, along these lines empowering you to all the more likely adjust working undertakings to their inclinations and to all the more likely propel them.

Social Skills

NLP gives a procedure to "getting in Rapport" with someone else. There are such a large number of ways that you can pick up compatibility with somebody and a considerable lot of them are oblivious, so you don't have the foggiest idea how you did it. In some cases you have compatibility and feel that vivacious association with individuals, and different occasions you don't. NLP Rapport process empowers you to intentionally comprehend what makes affinity and to deliberately make it, without fail!

NLP shows you how to assemble compatibility utilizing your breathing, the words that you use, the sentences that you build, how you hold you body. This empowers individuals to all the more likely impact others.

The advantages of creating enthusiastic insight utilizing NLP

There are immediate advantages in utilizing NLP to build up your enthusiastic insight, here is the thing that you will understanding:

Mindfulness – Improved fearlessness, genuineness

Self Regulation – Increased honesty and receptiveness to change

Inspiration – Optimism, solid drive to succeed and accomplish, improved duty

Sympathy – Improved capacity to work with others, construct incredible groups and hold the best individuals. Heavenly relational abilities

Social Skills – Increased capacity to impact and convince others, lead change.

What is NLP? These 4 methods could change how you think

Neuro-etymological programming (NLP) is frequently used to improve relational elements. It additionally has applications in self-awareness and improvement. A few NLP procedures can assist you with living a progressively charming and important life.

In fact, NLP underscores the significance of acing higher mindfulness strategies to spot examples, considerations, and suspicions that can be keeping you from discovering joy in your life. Here are four important NLP methods that you can utilize and the science behind them.

1. Mooring

Mooring is one the most well-known NLP strategies. The objective is to inspire positive reactions freely by partner a specific mental and passionate state to a grapple, which can be a picture, a word, or a motion. Tying down improves our capacity to control feelings and to play a functioning job in self-administration, making us less inclined to feeling feeble and overpowered.

Step by step instructions to utilize the mooring procedure

•Elicit when you encountered the extreme positive inclination you need to trigger in different circumstances (for example feeling accomplishment the minute you got an advancement).

•Bring in tactile prompts related with that state (for example what you saw, felt, smelt, heard).

•Bring the memory to its most extreme point and afterward partner your emotions to a stay (for example bend a ring on your finger, squeeze your ear cartilage).

- Take a brief break and rehash the means above.

- Test the stay (for example squeeze your ear cartilage) to inspire the extraordinary sentiment of accomplishment.

- You would then be able to utilize this strategy at whatever point you need an enthusiastic lift me-up, either all alone or close by other NLP procedures.

Securing depends on the mental idea of molding, whereby an upgrade triggers certain reactions. Tying down causes you evoke the reaction you need through redundancy. It benefits you by placing you accountable for your feelings. In addition, a few investigations propose that when combined with different methods and intercessions, securing can help defeat fears and silly feelings of trepidation.

2. Reframing

Next in the rundown of NLP methods is 'reframing', or review unfriendly occasions from an alternate 'outline'. This enables you to open up your psyche to circumstances that might be lying ahead as opposed to harping on the negatives. To put it plainly, reframing changes the concentration from negative and overwhelming to positive and enabled.

The most effective method to reframe an idea, feeling or conduct:

•Identify the idea, feeling or conduct you need to change.

•Establish contact with the deepest piece of yourself that is setting off the negative state of mind. This could be a picture, voice, an articulation, and so on.

•Find the positive aim behind that part. Suppose you have a dread of flying. The sound of a plane's motor taking off triggers tension since it needs to secure you. This goal is great, however the reaction is lacking.

- Focusing on the positive goal, attempt a few different ways of reacting that will assist you with acknowledging such aim. For instance, recognize the assurance and self-protection, which is the reason you pick the most secure method for voyaging (flying versus driving).

- Ensure your intuitive is completely dedicated to attempting elective reactions, and that it won't disrupt your reframing endeavors. Check for clashing convictions, and on and when you wind up rationalizing, return to stage four and discover elective methods for reacting.

Reframing is utilized as a restorative method for its capacity to change discernments. Various parts of the cerebrum trigger recollections and feelings: recollections are put away in the hippocampus, while the amygdala primarily controls feelings.

While reviewing past occasions, the amygdala reacts by setting off a feeling that duplicates the first one, however reframing helps us that the nature to remember that feeling isn't fixed and that we can break programmed designs and organize sound reactions over automatic responses. Reframing is one of those NLP systems that demonstrate it's conceivable to break free from the purported amygdala capture.

3. Meta-demonstrating

Meta-demonstrating is one of the most dominant NLP systems given its capacity to help distinguish willful limitations that might be keeping you from discovering bliss. The most straightforward approach to meta-model is by taking a gander at the language you use in regular daily existence, focusing on these three sorts of examples:

•Generalisations, prove in considerations along the lines of "I'm generally so unfortunate" or "all men are the equivalent."

•Distortions: mind perusing (for example "John didn't welcome me today, he should be annoyed with me") or cause-impact articulations (for example "in the event that I don't get in shape, I will feel like a disappointment").

•Deletions, or carefully selecting your comprehension of reality to affirm previous convictions. For example, somebody with poor confidence would disregard compliments and give undue consideration to scrutinizes, prompting contemplations like "individuals don't discover me appealing."

Instructions to utilize meta demonstrating:

Recognize which class your considerations have a place with, at that point start the exploratory procedure of scrutinizing the maladaptive idea design. For instance, in the event that you get yourself in an erasure like "individuals don't discover me appealing", meta-demonstrating inquiries to pose would be "which individuals explicitly?" and "how would you realize that?".

The odds are that your answers will incorporate a summed up proclamation with the words "consistently" or "never", at that point it's a great opportunity to ask yourself whether you are reasonable by asserting that things are consistently along these lines and never that way. When meta-displaying, it's additionally helpful to get some information about elective approaches. For instance, in the announcement "in the event that I don't get more fit, I'll feel like a disappointment", ask yourself in the case of feeling like a disappointment is your lone choice.

Meta-displaying works since it compels you to challenge imbued reaction designs that can develop into what specialists in mental science call over the top shirking conduct, which confines your capacity to gain from new encounters. The adequacy of this procedure is likewise connected to design division. At the point when looked with another circumstance, we will in general contrast and past ones, yet on and when example division is dynamic, you will comprehend that various situations require various reactions.

4. The Swish Method

This is one of the NLP methods that accentuate the seriously constraining impact of negative contemplations. The objective of the Swish strategy is to distinguish mental and passionate triggers of pessimism and supplant them with a perfect reaction. When utilizing the Swish procedure, you don't need to make any move, however become mindful of the options accessible and train your cerebrum to set off a "more joyful mode" at whatever point negative contemplations and feelings start to overwhelm you.

Step by step instructions to place the Swish Method enthusiastically:

•Identify the inclination that triggers nervousness. Model: you might be on edge about test execution despite the fact that you have given a valiant effort to get ready for it. For this situation, the trigger inclination would be anxiety and uneasiness.

•Next, know how your mind and body respond to such emotions (for example nail gnawing, hitches in the stomach, and so on.) Create a visual picture of the setting wherein this occurs (for example as you stroll into the test room).

•Think about how you might in a perfect world want to react as you physically enter the setting wherein the negative contemplations happen (for example certain, decidedly ready, idealistic, and so on.).

•This is known as the substitution suspected. In your psyche, envision the negative state and allegorically place the substitution thoroughly considered it, ensure it seems greater, more grounded, and increasingly energetic while causing the negative feeling to show up in highly contrasting or hazy.

As it occurs with other NLP systems for joy, you have to rehearse the Swish Method a couple of times to guarantee the substitution thought turns into the default reaction. Do it at any rate multiple times and accelerate the representation with each round. To check for viability, summon the trigger idea/feeling and its specific circumstance, and perceive how you feel about it.

The Swish Method is a representation procedure driven by the rule that truth can be stranger than fiction. Research examines have demonstrated that the mind doesn't separate among genuine and imagined occasions, as the two of them actuate similar pieces of the cerebrum. Different examines have indicated that the sort of mental practice associated with representation directly affects essential subjective aptitudes, including memory, consideration, and discernment. The advantages of acing this system incorporate improved enthusiastic execution and a quiet and certain methodology realizing that you don't have to give negative musings a chance to rule your life.

Chapter 7: Behavioral Traits And Character Quality Of The Manipulators

Some people are simply born manipulators blessed with the gift of the gab, and these natural-born manipulators all seem to share some common traits as described by a psychiatrist, Abigail Brenner.

They Are Incapable of True Altruism

Manipulative people hardly, if ever, do something out of the goodness of their hearts, there is usually an ulterior motive. For example, a manipulative person might buy you lunch today, and while you'd think that they were simply being generous, the aforementioned manipulative person would actually be planning to ask you to work one of their shifts tomorrow.

They're Big Talkers, But That Is Where It Ends

Manipulators do not usually follow up on their grandiose speeches or ideas with actual action. They build these incredible castles in the sky to draw you in, without the intention of ever acting on any of the commitments or promises they might make. For example, your boss may continually hint at a promotion before every big project they assign to you but has no intention to actually promote you. They're simply trying to manipulate you into giving 110% to a project in the hope of furthering your career.

They Are Not Empathetic

Manipulators either choose not to empathize with others or are simply incapable of empathy. You might spot a manipulator in this way, for example, when your company is undergoing downsizing. Under normal circumstances, even the employees who are not being laid off will feel sad and sorry for their colleagues who are losing their jobs, but a manipulator may be smug, or perhaps entirely apathetic, about their colleagues' misfortune.

They Are Better Gossips than Your Average High School Girl

Manipulators enjoy watching people squirm, and what better way to do this than by spreading malicious stories or by sharing the blunders of others with the world? Your colleague standing at the water cooler telling everyone about Sarah's divorce, and reveling in the gory details, might be revealing themselves to be a manipulator.

They Will Misuse Even the Smallest Kindness You Might Show Them

If you give manipulators an inch, they take a mile. Manipulators take advantage of people, it is simply what they do, and there's no easier way for them to do this than if you have already opened the door to their abuse by doing them a favor or by being kind to them. An example of this might be if you brought your coworker coffee for the morning meeting one day, and suddenly, this is what is expected of you, and now this coworker gets upset when they arrive at the meeting and their cup of coffee is not already waiting for them. This coworker might be a manipulator.

They Like To Play the Blame Game

Manipulators don't want to accept responsibility for their own wrongdoings, so they attempt to assign the blame to someone else, even if it means ruining that person's career, relationships, or friendships. An example of this might be that one coworker who made a blunder on a project they had been working on, but when confronted, they blamed the team leader for their failure or incompetence, resulting in their team leader losing their job. A manipulator would happily sacrifice somebody else's career in this way.

They Do Not Have Boundaries At All

Manipulators usually do not understand or do not care about the social contract prescribing the rules of etiquette to which the rest of us subscribe. A manipulator might ask you questions that are just a little too personal or might call you about a work-related matter at an unreasonable hour, or might show up at your house unexpectedly. They don't understand, or don't care about, the concept of being 'rude.'

They Are Unwilling To Compromise

It's their way or the highway. Manipulators insist on things being done exactly as they expect them to be done. Whether this is due to a need to insist on having authority, or whether this is an inborn defect that is unknown. And when they do not get their way, the resulting outburst is often incredibly aggressive and explosive. For this reason, people are often wary of going against a manipulator, which is why so many of them allegedly end up in higher management positions.

They Think That They Are Very Important

Psychopaths tend to have a grandiose sense of self, and often think of themselves as the center of the universe. As a result of this inflated ego, psychopaths often demand special, or superior, treatment. They expect to be treated like the royalty they believe themselves to be, and all hell breaks loose when their incredibly high standards are not met.

They Are Incapable of Feeling Guilt or Remorse

Psychopaths do not have a conscience. They are able to contemplate things that would make others rile back in disgust, gagging at the very thought. Psychopaths are often born with an underdeveloped or maldeveloped frontal lobe, impacting their ability to feel empathy or understand what is morally right or wrong. As a result of this, they are often capable of acts of incredible cruelty.

They Are Master Manipulators

Here, you can refer back to the common traits of manipulators listed above. Psychopaths are fantastically talented at guilt-tripping others, and equally gifted at flattery and seduction. You might find yourself unknowingly, or unwittingly, obeying a psychopath's every command due to their ability to manipulate.

They Are Incredibly Charming

This slots into the flattery and seduction mentioned above. Psychopaths are very good at getting people to be 'on their team.' They smile and joke their way into the lives of the people around you, and these people are often unable to see the psychopath for what they truly are. A psychopath will have the entire neighborhood wrapped around their finger in no time. They might even get elected for office.

They Are Also Incredibly Ruthless

You will absolutely know if you have crossed a psychopath in some way as they are likely to reciprocate through small (or large) acts of revenge. They are also more than happy to turn those who are nearest and dearest to you against you if they feel that you have wronged them in some way. A psychopath usually dispenses his or her own justice, usually with disastrous effects.

They Are Irresponsible and Have No Regard for the Safety of Others

A prime example of this is the Wall Street bankers who toppled the United States into an economic crisis in 2008 due to underhanded hedge fund trading with derivatives. Many of them were aware that they would be driving others to bankruptcy, but still went ahead and did it for their own personal gain.

They Violate the Rights of Others

An example of this would be the case of Robert Maxwell, the incredibly wealthy publishing giant, who, after his death, was found to have stolen millions by defrauding the pension funds of thousands of innocent people.

They Engage In Socially Irresponsible Behavior like Binge Drinking, Addiction to Narcotics, Promiscuous Sexual Activity, Or Other Criminal Activities

An example of a psychopath engaging in socially irresponsible (or rather, reprehensible) behavior is Ted Bundy, the infamous serial killer and promising law student who confessed to murdering 30 women in his spare time.

They Are Frequently In Trouble with the Law

This happens as a natural consequence of socially irresponsible behavior and violating the rights of others. Psychopaths are not always caught red-handed for murder, though sometimes, these transgressions are as small as not believing that the speed limit applies to them, thus amassing a small mountain of fines.

They Like to Hurt Others and Are Often Sadists

An example of this is Ilse Koch, the wife of a Nazi secret service member, who would walk around naked in a Jewish concentration camp and had any man who so much as dared to glance at her shot on the spot.

An Inability To, or Apathy Toward, Understanding Right from Wrong

Psychopaths either do not care about doing the right thing or do not know that they are doing the wrong thing. An example of this is the 'angel of mercy' stereotype found within the study of criminology. Offenders who fall under this stereotype commit murders with the belief that they are doing the victim a favor by euthanizing them.

The Need to Fix and Heal Those around Them

Those who are easy to manipulate are always on the lookout for someone down on their luck to help out of the gutter. The reason this makes them easy to manipulate is that absolutely anybody can pretend to be going through a hard time, and in doing so win the loyalty and trust of the aforementioned person.

An Inability To Set Boundaries or To Say 'No'

Those who are easy to manipulate are generally so scared of confrontation that they are not willing to spark an argument by being resistant or by voicing their opinion. This specific trait is easy to exploit for obvious reasons. If they just cannot say no, you can burden them with favors and expectations, and anticipate no resistance in return.

Chapter 8: How To Manipulate

Manipulation is, in essence, the art of deception. And, as it is an art, it is teachable—and something which you can learn to master.

There are almost an infinite number of psychological manipulation techniques; however, only the most successfully employed techniques will be discussed in this chapter.

The first psychological manipulation technique we'll examine is known as the **fear-then-relief** method. In his 2007 novel, The Science of Social Influence, Anthony Pratkanis explains that this technique involves eliciting an extreme fear response from your subject, and then quickly and abruptly relieving this fear. The minute the subject exits the shroud of fear that the manipulator has imbibed them with, they are disarmed. This moment of pliability happens when the subject's mind tries to process whatever just happened. Pratkanis's book also cites a study which supports this method's efficacy. During this experiment, shoppers were tapped on the shoulder while perusing the store's shelves by a strange blind man. The tap on the shoulder made them jump, but realizing that it had only been a blind man wanting to ask the time immediately relieved their fear. After this encounter, the scientists conducting the study tried to sell the shoppers a political postcard. The shoppers who had experienced the encounter with the blind man were more likely to buy the postcard than the control group of shoppers, who were less interested in the purchase.

This technique is easy to apply in real-life scenarios. For example, you could tell a coworker, "Our boss noticed you left early on Thursday... but don't worry, I covered for you." The theory is that directly after using a sentence similar to this, your communicative partner should be more receptive to commands.

The next technique is called the **social exchange**, and is basically a well-thought-out guilt trip. Richard Perloff first described this as a manipulation technique in his book, The Dynamics of Persuasion. A social exchange is like an unwritten social contract. Most cultures prime us to accept "tit for tat," and thus, once someone has done us a favor, we feel indebted to them. You can use this to your advantage.

A real-life example of this would be reminding a coworker of a favor you did for them ("Remember when I covered for you last Thursday?") before asking for something in return. He suggests that after being reminded of the favor you did him or her, your coworker is more likely to be compliant with a request.

The **foot-in-the-door** technique was first described by Johnathan Freedman and Scott Fraser in their 1996 study, Compliance Without Pressure: The Foot in the Door Technique. This technique essentially entails asking a small favor of someone, and after this favor has been granted, asking a second, larger favor. Freedman and Scott believed that after agreeing to comply with the first request, a person would be more likely to agree to the second. An example of this, which you may have personally experienced already, would be when a homeless person asks you for directions, and upon receiving them from you, asks for $10. Theoretically, you are more likely to offer the $10 if you had agreed to give the directions first. You could apply this technique at work, for example, by asking your coworker to check your emails for you. Once they have complied, you could then, in theory, ask them to reply to a customer query in your inbox, and they would be more likely to agree.

Another infamous manipulation technique is **blame shifting**, also known as **projection**. This is one of the seedier manipulation techniques available to manipulators, but it is very effective. Human beings are programmed to want to assign blame to someone, or something, for nearly any unfortunate circumstance that could befall us—and we are particularly receptive to being told who is to blame, instead of ascertaining it for ourselves. This is also responsible for the phenomenon known as a "witch hunt."

You can use this propensity to assign blame to your own advantage. When stuck in a situation in which you are "in trouble" (whether this is with a romantic partner, a friend or your boss), it is best to choose a new suspect to blame for whatever misfortune you may have caused and single them out to the person confronting you. Human nature will push them to accept whomever you have assigned blame to as the guilty party. You could even shift the blame onto the person who is confronting you without this technique losing its efficacy.

But blame shifting is not the only technique available to master manipulators. Its cousin, **gaslighting**, is pretty effective, too. Gaslighting is a psychological manipulation technique in which the manipulator, in essence, drives the recipient to doubt his or her own sanity, perception of reality, or memory.

Gaslighting is a long-term manipulation technique, so it generally requires a bit of commitment.

The first step of gaslighting is to isolate the victim from friends and family—you essentially need to be their only contact with the world. This can be done by causing them to doubt their friends' intentions and motives, or by causing a rift in their relationships through some other means. Once you have someone isolated, you basically control how they see and interact with the world.

The second step is to gain the victim's trust by opening up to them. Tell them your deepest, darkest secrets—they don't necessarily have to be true—and the victim will almost immediately feel a sense of trust in you. This doesn't mean you should run up to strangers and confess that you killed the family cat—the secret to this is timing. Open up to the victim when it is appropriate. This means that you will need to foster at least some kind of reciprocal relationship with the person you intend to manipulate.

The third step is to be nice—at least, at first. The trick is to be kind to the victim until they begin to crave your affection. It is at this point that you can either maintain the relationship or, if your motives are darker, slowly withdraw your affection. The recipient is more likely to be loyal toward the manipulator if they feel affection toward them, and will theoretically be even more complacent should the manipulator slowly start to deprive them of this affection.

The fourth step is projection, as described earlier in this chapter. It is important that you do not allow the victim to see any fault in you. A good manipulator needs to be squeaky clean and blameless. When hiccups do arise in your relationship with the recipient, it is important that you assign the blame to someone other than yourself. Once again, the blame can even be shifted onto the recipient themselves, in this scenario.

The final step is to warp the victim's sense of reality or self. Manipulators do this by telling their recipients that they are simply imagining things, that they are overreacting, or that their emotional response is not appropriate even when it is. If the above four steps have been completed successfully, the manipulator should be able to cause the recipient to believe that they are going crazy or that their perceptions of the world are invalid altogether.

Chapter 9: Dark Persuasion Methods

Trigger methods are often used by other names and are called forced strategies and stimulating tactics. There is only one way to convince someone to think or act in a particular way, which by persuasion. Persuasion can talk to the subject while providing evidence. To change the mind of the object, they can use some kind of force or pull on the object. And they can do some service for this problem or use different tactics. This section details the different stimulation modes available for each method and their effectiveness.

Use of violence

In some situations, persuaders may decide that it is better to use some form of violence to reflect on the problem. This can happen if the ideas don't fit properly, if regular conversations don't work, or if the agency is fit. Dissatisfaction or regret about the mode of conversation. Violence is often used as a kind of horror tactic because the topic has less time to think logically than during normal conversation.

Coercion is often used when persuader has little success with other coercions. However, violence may be available. Otherwise, you can use violence when the agent feels out of control or when the agent provides contradictory evidence, and the agent is angry.

Using violence with respect to violence is often not the best idea

For the stimulation process. This is because many subjects view the use of violence as a threat because they have no choice but to require the use of violence. The attraction you want is to choose a path to the lesson, but as power is added to the mix, you lose the freedom to choose. Instead of feeling threatened. If the material is perceived as intimidating, the agent is less likely to hear or think about the agent. For these reasons, the use of violence in the area of coercion is generally not recommended and not avoided. Different from other mental controls.

Influence weapon

Another method that can be used to convince a subject to lean in a particular way is to use available impact weapons. Robert Chardini created these six influences in his influential book. Techniques of persuasion have six goals. Persuaders can accomplish these. The six weapons of influence are reciprocity, commitment and persistence, social evidence, empathy, empowerment, and lack. It is very important that the agent is part of these six influential weapons

Mutually

The first weapon of influence is mutual politics. The principle is that when a persuader offers something to another person. If there is a value, the object tries to return the agent. This means that a persuader occasionally feels obliged to perform a similar service for the agent when a persuader provides a service in a matter. Although the two services are not the same, they are the same.

Everybody is equal.

The tour ultimately creates a sense of duty for the subject and can be a powerful tool if persuader wants to use the trigger. Interactive rules are very useful as they help the agent get the subject in the right mood for coercion. Inject the sense of duty into this thing and drown it. In this case, a feeling of duty tends to make persuader believe that they will act or behave in a certain way.

Another advantage of persuader is the use of interactions

A moral position to impose obligations on objects; This is a position supported by social norms. Persuader does not have to worry about whether there is an appropriate code of ethics to return the favor. If the subject does not consider this necessary, persuader has various tools at its disposal to implement them. As a community, people hate people who don't pay back or pay for free gifts and services. If persuader doesn't feel that classes are going to and from them, they can involve them in their social group.

You can do this by telling other friends and colleagues how you like the topic. However, the material will not be returned if necessary. Persuader is now promoting socialization classes by turning to helpers, further increasing their chances of persuading them to do something.

In most cases, the lessons are readily returned to the agent

Without the need for external strength. If it is found, the agent looks for ways to repay the agent. The score becomes uniform and does not appear greedy or selfish. Persuaders can provide an easy solution to repay these debts. The lessons appreciate this simple solution, and persuader is more likely to do what they want.

Commitment and sustainability

The next weapon of influence discussed is commitment and sustainability. Persuader must use both if they want to persuade someone to change. From their point of view. When things are smooth, they are easy to understand, and the lessons help them improve their results. It does not change the fact that persuaders always use it or change other information that requires material to process. Instead of helping. The process of persuasion, which maintains consistency, makes the agent look like a liar or an untrustworthy person, which leads to the failure of the induction process.

One of the most important aspects of the stimulus process is persistence.

Reason:

Hard work is invaluable in society: in most cases, people want things to be a certain way.

There are many types of everyday life, but people believe that the whole thing is more consistent.

They can remember what happened, know what to expect, and be prepared for change. If there is no consistency available, it is very difficult to plan things,

It is always a confusing problem. If you want to believe in a topic, you need to make sure your facts are consistent and meaningful.

Stable

It benefits the everyday attitude of most people. Have you ever tried to plan a day when something unexpected happens? It makes things almost impossible and ends. Feel like a disaster. People love patience because they know what to expect and what to do.

They know when to eat when to work and when to do other things.

Stability provides an invaluable summary of the issues of modern existence. Life is enough without it

Then add those that aren't. If people can live a sustainable life, things will be much easier.

Sustainability is a great tool because it can make the right decisions and process information. If so, the agent wants to successfully persuade the topic. He needs to make sure the message is consistent. There is no room for false evidence to appear later and destroy the entire process. Keep the facts true and accurate, and believe that the topic is very good.

Related to permanence is engagement. It takes some commitment to know that the title is really concrete and worth the effort. Advertising means buying a product, and politics means voting for product-specific candidates. Commitment depends on the type of trust. Under the concept of sustainability, a person may value a commitment if involved in writing or verbally turned out to be more true written duties, titles can be very psychologically specific, and there is solid evidence that they have agreed to the promise. It makes every sense. Many people verbally promise, fix, or do something, but they don't. Of course, some people will do what they said.

You are more likely to make verbal promises than if you do not, but often it is difficult to achieve the desired result. Furthermore, there is no way to confirm this because there is only one verbal agreement, there is disagreement, and no one can win. On the other hand, if the agent can confirm in writing, they have enough evidence that the thing is over.

It is very important that persuader agrees to the obligation, as subjects are more likely to act in a manner that meets this obligation when a new approach is committed. Afterward, the important thing is that the topic continues, and you can convince yourself of this. You and others will provide a variety of reasons and reasons to support your involvement to avoid agent problems. If the agent can solve the problem in that location, there is little that the agent has to do.

Social evidence

Stimulation is a form of social interaction, so it must follow the social rules that occur. This thing is influenced by those around you. What they want others to do instead of doing it themselves. In classes are based on their beliefs and actions, what others around them do, how the same people behave, and how they feel. For example, if your subject grew up in a city, you behave more like the rest of the neighborhood. On the other hand, those who grew up in a very religious community

Time to pray, learn, and help others.

With this belief, the term "power of the crowd" is very useful. Classes always want to know what others are doing around them. It is almost hysterical to do what others do in this country. How people differ and what they want to be as individuals must agree.

Examples of what people do are heard on the phone because other people are doing something. Host "Waiting for the operator; please call now." You can feel like an operator is sitting there doing nothing because nobody is calling. This makes it more difficult for them to make a call because they should not make a call when there is no one on the phone. The host changes only a few words, and instead: "If the operator is busy, call again." Very different results. Here the Chancellor assumes that the operator calls several clients. The system must, therefore, be appropriate and systematic. Subjects are more likely to make calls regardless of whether they pass or need to be suspended immediately.

Induction technology

The effects of social evidence can be very useful in situations where the object is uncertain, or there are many similarities to the situation. In ambiguous or uncertain situations with many choices or possibilities, the subjects often choose what others are doing. The decisions are very similar, so they all work, but assume that the decisions made by others are correct. Another way to use social evidence is with some similarities. For example, classes are about some people, and they are more likely to change. If someone resembles a responsible person, the person is more likely to listen to and follow them than the responsible person is very different. Persuaders can use social resource ideas to support the process of coercion. You are the first way to do this

Look at the words they say. In the Game Show example, the two quotes were the same, but changing the words had two different meanings. Both are wrong. You have triggered a variety of reactions. When persuader can see their words from things, they can get the right answer from the subject and force the subject to adopt the same ideas and beliefs.

In addition, persuaders will be more successful if they are able to share ideas with people like themselves. That is why politicians want to fight in groups for similar ideas. If you want to reach larger groups, change your ideas to address these new groups. Cause or that; if the subject wants a persuader, they are more likely to say yes. There are two main factors that influence a material agent's preference. The first is physical attraction, and the second is unity first if the agent is physically very attractive in this regard.

Changing the attitude of others makes it easier for you to get what you want, so you will feel confident. This fascinating factor has been shown to be effective in transmitting cheap messages and other attributes of the agent, such as intelligence, kindness, and ability. that is

All work together to increase the likelihood of attractive people easily believing in the topic. The second element, unity, is a bit easier. The idea is that if the title resembles a persuader, you are more likely to say yes to what the agent wants. That is, the process is very natural, and in most cases, persuader does not need to consider whether it is right.

One way for persuaders to convince their problem is to take power. Most people believe that what experts say about a subject is true. Most likely to ask a trusted and knowledgeable agent for the topic. This means that if a persuader can bring these two things to the table, he has already been guided to believe his claim. The research was done to show how this powerful technique could convince persuaders to listen.

If persuader wants to convince them, they need to develop some techniques to help them. The subjects are subjected to various types of coercion every day. The food manufacturer is trying to buy lessons. The studio advertises the latest blockbusters, but there are also new and old ones. With stimulation found almost everywhere, persuaders can find it challenging to find ways to look at an object. Reliable techniques have been observed and studied. This can be very useful for different people many years ago. Systematic research into these techniques began early and grew the 20th century. Because the ultimate goal of persuasion is to convince the subject to present a convincing argument; If you accept it and adopt it as a new approach, it is worth finding out which forced technique is most successful.

Create needs

One way persuader can change their mind is to create needs or address existing needs. If done correctly, address this type of trust issue. Ie, For persuader to be successful, they need to address the basic needs of the problem. You need self-realization, self-esteem, love, food, and shelter. The reason this method works so well for persuader is that it really needs these things. Eating is not something that can survive Not too long. If persuader believes their business is the best, or change their beliefs, they are more likely to get more food in the shelter or succeed.

Appeal to the social needs of materials. Social needs are not as effective as primary needs, but they are still important tools to use. People like and want to be part of the crowd. They like the kiwi ritual. Some products can give them and feel that they belong to a higher social status—ideas to appeal to them. The social needs of the title can be found in current TV commercials. In these ads, viewers are asked to buy an item, which makes them known or similar to others.

As persuaders address the subject's social needs, they may reach new areas of interest to the subject. When it comes to coercion, choosing a language can make a big difference. There are many ways to say the same thing, one may promote this, but the other does not. Say the right words and the right words.

When forced, that method makes all the difference. Stimulation is a powerful mind-control tool that is often underestimated. I did not notice. Perhaps this gives you more topic choices than other forms of mental control. With other options, persuader may be forced to submit in private, with little choice as to what will eventually happen in the process. Regarding trust, facts are presented. Decisions can be made even if facts are presented in the best possible way in a certain way

Chapter 10: A Quick Intro On Brainwashing

Through the media and the motion pictures that are seen, numerous individuals consider mentally conditioning to be an insidious practice that is finished by the individuals who are attempting to degenerate, impact, and to pick up power. Some who truly put stock in the intensity of mentally conditioning accept that individuals surrounding them are attempting to control their brains and their conduct.

Generally, the way toward mental conditioning happens in a substantially more unpretentious manner and does not include the vile practices that the vast majority partner with it. This section will go into significantly more insight regarding what mentally conditioning is and how it can impact the subject's perspective. What is mentally conditioning? Mentally conditioning in this manual will be talked about as far as its utilization in brain science. In this connection, mentally conditioning is alluded to as a technique for idea change through social impact.

This sort of social impact is happening all for the duration of the day to each individual, paying little heed to whether they understand it or not. Social impact is the accumulation of techniques that are utilized so as to change other individuals' practices, convictions, and frames of mind.

For instace, consistency techniques that are utilized in the working environment could actually be viewed as a type of mentally cnditioning since they expect you to act and think a particular way when you are on employment.

Mentally programming can turn out to be all the more a social issue in its most extreme structure in light of the fact that these methodologies work at changing the manner in which somebody supposes without the subject consenting to it.

Brainwashing Techniques

For mentally conditioning to work adequately, the subject is going to need to experience a total disconnection and reliance because of its intrusive impact regarding the matter. This is one reason that a significant number of the mentally programming cases that is thought about happening in totalistic cliques or jail camps. The brainwasher, or the operator, must most likely oversee their subject.

This implies they should control the dietary patterns, resting designs, and satisfying the other human needs of the subject and none of these activities can happen without the desire of the specialist. During this procedure, the operator will work to deliberately separate the subject's entire personality to fundamentally make it not work right any longer.

When the personality is broken, the operator will work to supplant it with the ideal convictions, dispositions, and practices. The way toward mental programming is still begging to be proven wrong whether it will work.

Most analysts hold the convictions that it is conceivable to mentally program a subject as long as the correct conditions are available. That being said, the entire procedure isn't as serious as it is exhibited in the media.

There are likewise various meanings of mental conditioning that make it increasingly hard to decide the impacts of indoctrinating regarding the matter. A portion of these definitions requires that there must be a type of danger to the physical body of the subject so as to be viewed as mentally conditioning. This definition, at that point, even the practices done by numerous fanatic factions would not be viewed as obvious mentally programming as no physical maltreatment happens.

Different meanings of mental conditioning will depend on control and pressure without physical power so as to get the adjustment in the convictions of the subjects. In any case, specialists accept that the impact of mentally programming, even under the perfect conditions, is just a transient event.

They accept that the old character of the subject isn't totally destroyed with the training; rather, it is put into stowing away and will return once the new personality isn't strengthened any longer. Robert Jay Lifton concocted some intriguing considerations on indoctrinating with regards to the 1950s after he contemplated detainees of the Chinese and Korean War camps. During his perceptions, he verified that these detainees experienced a multistep procedure to indoctrinating.

This procedure started with assaults on the feeling of self with the detainee and afterward finished with an alleged change in convictions of the subject. There are 10 stages that Lifton characterized for the mentally programming procedure in the subjects that he considered. These included:

An ambush on the character of the subject

Forcing blame regarding the matter

Forcing the subject into self-selling out

Reaching a limit

Offering the subject mercy on the off chance that they change

Compulsion to admit

Channeling the blame the planned way

Releasing the subject of assumed blame

Progressing to agreement

The last admission before a resurrection.

These stages must occur in a zone that is in finished disengagement. This implies the majority of the typical social references that the subject is accustomed to interacting with are inaccessible.

Likewise, mind blurring strategies will be utilized so as to speed up the procedure, for example, lack of healthy sustenance and lack of sleep. While this probably won't be valid for all mentally programming cases, regularly there is a nearness of some kind of physical mischief which adds to the objective experiencing issues in speculation autonomously and fundamentally like they typically would.

Steps Utilized

While Lifton isolated the means of the mentally programming procedure into 10 stages, present-day analysts arrange it into three phases so as to more readily comprehend what continues for the subject during this procedure.

These three phases incorporate the separating of oneself, acquainting the possibility of salvation with the subject, and the modifying of the self of the subject. Seeing every one of these stages and the procedure that occurs with every one of them can assist you with understanding what is going the personality of the subject with this procedure.

Breaking Down of Self

The primary phase of the mentally conditioning procedure is simply the separating of them. During this procedure, the operator needs to separate the old character of the subject so as to make them feel increasingly defenseless and open to the ideal new personality. This progression is vital so as to proceed on the procedure.

The specialist won't be fruitful with their undertakings if the subject is still solidly set in their determination and their old personality. Separating this personality and making the individual inquiry the things around them can make it simpler to change the character in the later advances. This is done through a few stages including a strike on the character of the subject, bringing on blame, self-disloyalty, and after that achieving the limit.

Assault on Identity

The strike on the personality of the subject is essentially the orderly assault regarding the matters' feeling of self or their inner self or character alongside their center arrangement of conviction. It makes the subject inquiry their identity by making them feel that all that they have ever known isn't right.

In detainee camps, for instance, the operator will say things like "You are not safeguarding opportunity," "You are not a man," and "You are not an officer."

The subject will be under assaults like these always for a considerable length of time up to months. This is done so as to debilitate the subjects so they become bewildered, confounded, and depleted. At the point when the subject achieves this sort of express, their convictions will begin to appear to be less strong and they may begin to accept the things that they are told.

Blame

When the subject has experienced the attack on their character, they will enter the phase of blame. The subject will be always informed that they are terrible while experiencing this new character emergency that has been expedited.

This is done so as to expedite an enormous feeling of blame to the subject. The subject will be always enduring an onslaught for any of the things that they have done, paying little respect to how enormous or little the demonstrations might be.

The scope of the assaults can change also; the subject could be reprimanded for their convictions frameworks to the manner in which they dress and even on the grounds those they eat too gradually. After some time, the subject is going to begin to feel disgrace around them constantly and they will feel that every one of the things they are doing aren't right. This can make them feel increasingly defenseless and prone to oblige the new personality the specialist needs to deliver.

Self-disloyalty

Since the subject has been persuaded that they are awful and that the majority of their activities are bothersome, the specialist is getting down to business to drive the subject to concede that they are awful. Now, the subject is suffocating in their own blame and feeling exceptionally muddled. Through the continuation of the psychological assaults, the danger of some incredible physical damage, or a blend of the two, the operator will almost certainly power the subject to upbraid his old character.

This can incorporate a wide assortment of things, for example, getting the subject to upbraid their very own companions, companions, and family who offer a similar conviction framework as them. While this procedure may require a significant stretch of time to happen, when it does, the subject will feel like he double-crossed those that he feels faithful to. This will expand the disgrace just as the loss of character that the objective is as of now feeling, further separating the personality of the subject.

Limit

By this point, the subject is feeling very separated and bewildered. They might pose inquiries, for example, where am I. Who am I? What's more, what would it be a good idea for me to do? The subject is in a character emergency now and is experiencing some profound disgrace. Since they have double-crossed the majority of the convictions and the general population that he has constantly known, the subject will experience a mental meltdown.

In psychology research, this fair method an accumulation of serious side effects that regularly show an enormous number of assumed mental aggravations. A portion of the side effects can include general bewilderment, profound sadness, and uncontrolled wailing. The subject may have the sentiments of being totally lost alongside having a freehold on the real world.

When the subject achieves this limit, they will have lost their feeling of self and the specialist will basically have the option to do anything they desire with them now since the subject has lost their comprehension of what is happening around them and their identity. Likewise now, the specialist will set up the different allurements that are fundamental so as to change over the subject towards another conviction framework. The new framework will be set up in a manner to offer salvation to the subject from the wretchedness that they are feeling.

Possibility of Salvation

This progression includes offering the subject the likelihood of salvation just in the event that they are happy to get some distance from their previous conviction framework and rather grasp the enhanced one that is being advertised.

The subject is allowed to comprehend what is around them, is informed that they would be great again and that they would feel good on the off chance that they would simply pursues the new wanted way. There are four stages that are incorporated into this phase of the mentally programming procedure; mercy, impulse to admission, directing of the blame and discharging of the blame.

Compulsion to Confession

When the specialist has had the option to pick up the trust of their subject, they will attempt to get an admission out of the procedure. This stage is regularly known as the "You can support yourself." During this phase of the mentally conditioning procedure, the subject begins to see the contrasts between the torments and blame that they felt during the character ambush and the alleviation that they are feeling from the unexpected mercy that is advertised.

In the event that the indoctrinating procedure is compelling, the subject may even begin to feel a longing to respond to a portion of the consideration that has been offered to them by the specialist. At the point when this happens, the specialist will almost certainly present the possibility of admission as a potential way to alleviating the subject of the torment and blame that they are feeling. The subject will at that point be driven through a procedure of admitting the majority of the wrongs and sins that they have done previously.

Obviously, these wrongs and sins will be in connection with how they influence the new personality that is being made. For instance, if the subject is wartime captive, this progression will enable them to admit the wrongs that they did by protecting opportunity or battling against the routine of the other nation. Regardless of whether these are not really wrongs or sins, they conflict with the new philosophy that the routine is in every case right thus they should be admitted.

Directing of Blame

When the subject enters the directing of blame advance, they have been experiencing the strike of their self for a long time. When the subject achieves this point in the indoctrinating procedure, they can feel the blame and the disgrace that has been put on them, yet it has practically lost its significance. They are not ready to let you know precisely what they have fouled up to make them feel along these lines; they simply realize that they are incorrect.

The specialist will most likely utilize the clean slate of the subject so as to clarify why they are in the torment that they are feeling. The operator will almost certainly connect the feeling of blame that the subject is feeling to anything they desire.

This is where the agreement between the old convictions and the new convictions are built up; essentially, the old conviction framework has been set up to compare with the mental distress that the subject has been feeling while the new conviction framework has been set up to relate with the capacity to get away from that anguish. The decision will be the subjects', yet it is really simple to see that they would pick the new framework so as to begin feeling good.

Discharging of Blame

In this progression, the subject has come to understand that their old qualities and convictions uncovered causing them torment. At this point, they are worn out and tired of inclination the blame and disgrace that has been put on them for a long time. They begin to understand that it isn't really something that they have done that makes them feel thusly; rather, it is their convictions that are causing the blame. The troubled subject can feel some help from the way that there is something that they can do about the blame.

They will likewise feel calm on the grounds that they presently have gone to the understanding that they are not the terrible individual, rather the general population they have been near and their conviction framework that is the genuine guilty party that is causing the disquietude which is something that they can fix so as to turn out to be great once more.

The subject has discovered that they have a way to get out basically by getting away from the off-base conviction framework that they have held and grasping the enhanced one that is being advertised. All that the subject should do so as to discharge the blame that they are feeling is to revile the foundations and individuals that are related with the old conviction framework and after that, they will be discharged from the blame.

The subject presently has some command over this stage. They will probably understand that the arrival of blame is up to them totally. All the subject should accomplish for this phase so as to be discharged from the misleading quality is to admit to any of the demonstrations they have submitted that are related to the old conviction framework.

When the full admission is done, the subject will have finished the full mental dismissal of their previous character. The operator should venture in now so as to offer another personality to the subject and help them to modify their character into the ideal one.

Rebuilding of Self

By these steps, the subject has experienced a ton of steps and enthusiastic strife. They have been put through an experience that is intended to strip them of their old character, told that they are awful and should be fixed, and gradually go to the acknowledgment that their conviction framework is the reason for their misleading quality and that it should be changed. When the majority of this has been achieved, the subject is going to need to figure out how to remake their self, with the assistance of the operator.

This stage permits the specialist the opportunity to embed the thoughts of the new framework since the subject is a fresh start and anxious to figure out how to be and feel good. There are two stages that are seen during this stage including amicability and the last admission before beginning once again.

Final Confession and Starting Over

Despite the fact that the decision is truly not theirs by any means, the specialist has deliberately worked the entire time to lead the subject to feeling like they have the through and through freedom to pick the new character. On the off chance that the mentally programming procedure is done effectively, the subject will ponder the new decisions and establish that the best one is to take up the new character.

They have been adapted to think along these lines and in their new perspective, the one bodes well. There are no different decisions; picking the new personality enables them to be soothed from the blame that they feel and prompts satisfaction while picking the old character prompts torment and blame.

There would be backtracking in the entire mentally programming procedure and they would be compelled to experience everything again so as to finish up with the ideal outcomes. During this phase of the procedure, the subject gets the opportunity to conclude that they will pick well, which implies that they get the opportunity to go with the new character.

At the point when the subject differences the distress and torment of their old personality with the quietness that accompanies the new, they will pick the new character. This new character resembles a type of salvation. The thing encourages them to feel better and not need to manage blame and misery any longer. As this stage finishes, the subject is going to dismiss their old character and will experience a procedure of vowing faithfulness to their new one realizing that it will work at improving their life.

Ordinarily, there are services and ceremonies that happen during this last stage. The change from the old personality to the new character is a major ordeal since much time and vitality has been utilized on the two sides. During these functions, the subject will be enlisted into the new network and grasped with the new personality. For some indoctrinating unfortunate casualties, there is the sentiment of resurrection during this period.

You are permitted to grasp your new character and are greeted wholeheartedly into the new network that is presently your own. Rather than being disengaged and alone, you have numerous new companions and network individuals on your side. Rather than inclination the blame and torment that has tormented you for a long time you are going to feel joy and serenity with everything that is around you. The new character is currently yours and the mentally conditioning change is finished.

This procedure can occur over a time of numerous months to even years. The vast majority are set in their personality and the convictions that they have; change the majority of this in only a couple of days except if the individual was at that point willing to change and that would make the mentally conditioning procedures superfluous. Seclusion would likewise be important in light of the fact that outside impacts will keep the subject from depending on the operator during this procedure.

This is the reason the greater part of the indoctrinating cases happen in jail camps and other disengaged cases; by far most of the individuals won't get the opportunity of experiencing mentally conditioning because of the way that they are constantly encompassed by individuals and innovation that would obstruct the entire indoctrinating process.

When the individual is in detachment, the procedure takes quite a while because of the numerous means that must be taken so as to change the beliefs held by the person for a long time with the goal that they will hold onto the new way of life as their own while additionally feeling that the decision has dependably been theirs.

As can be seen, there are many advances that must be taken so as to experience the mentally programming procedure. It isn't something that will happen just by running into somebody in the city and trading a couple of words.

It requires the segregation and time to persuade the subject that all that they know isn't right and that they are a terrible individual. It at that point proceeds with attempting to power out an admission that the subject is awful and that they need to deny everything that they have done that is awful because of their old personality.

At long last, the subject will be driven toward accepting that they can improve on the off chance that they simply surrender their old thoughts and rather grasp the tranquility and rightness that accompanies the new personality that is introduced. These means must happen for the indoctrinating to be viable and the new character to be set up.

Basic Strategies Utilized in mentally programming

Mentally conditioning isn't generally as exceptional as what has been depicted so far in this part. The strategies portrayed are utilized for "genuine mentally programming" and are once in a while done to the subject. There are numerous different kinds of mentally programming that really occur on an everyday premise. They probably won't work to make you totally surrender your old character for another one, yet they do work to help move your contemplations and thoughts on what is happening around you. This segment is going to concentrate on a portion of the strategies that are frequently utilized during the indoctrinating procedure, paying little heed to whether it is genuine mentally conditioning or not.

Entrancing spellbinding, which will be examined in more detail in the following section, is a type of indoctrinating in certain conditions. Mesmerizing is fundamentally the acceptance of a high condition of suggestibility. This state is regularly masked daintily as reflection or unwinding. During the procedure of spellbinding, the specialist can propose things to the subject in order to get them to act or respond with a particular goal in mind.

Numerous individuals know about trance from the stage demonstrates they have seen. It is additionally regularly utilized as an approach to improve wellbeing.

Companion Weight everybody has an inborn need to have a place. This could be with a specific gathering, their family, companions, and the network. With the friend weight strategy, there is a concealment of the uncertainty that the subject feels alongside disposing of their protection from new thoughts by misusing this olid need to have a place. Whenever done right, the subject might be all the more eager to evaluate new things, be less modest around new individuals, and may have a simpler time making new companions.

Love Bombarding—the feeling of family is solid in individuals. This is the gathering that you were naturally introduced to and that you have as far as anyone knows been around for as long as you can remember. They realize you superior to anything anybody and the individuals who have passed up this sort of relationship may find that they are feeling alone and undesirable.

With affection shelling, the operator can make a feeling of the family by the utilization of enthusiastic holding, feeling and through sharing and physical touch.

This enables the specialist and the subject to bond in a familial manner, making it simpler to exchange the old character for the enhanced one.

Dismissing Old Qualitiess referenced somewhat prior in this section, the operator is attempting to persuade the subject to reprove the majority of their own qualities. This procedure is quickened through the procedure of terrorizing, physical risk, and different methods. Toward the end, the subject will censure the qualities and convictions that they once held close and will start to acknowledge the new way of life that is exhibited to them by the operator.

Befuddling Principle in this strategy, there will be a support to indiscriminately acknowledge the new personality while dismissing other rationales that the subject will have. So as to do this, the specialist will experience a mind-boggling set of addresses about a precept that will be boundless. The subject will figure out how to aimlessly confide in what the specialist is stating through this procedure, regardless of whether it is about the regulation or about the new personality that is being framed.

Meta correspondence—this strategy is utilized when the specialist attempts to embed subliminal messages into the psyche of the subject. This will be done when the specialist focuses on specific words or expressions that are vital to the new character. These expressions and catchphrases will be embedded into confounding long addresses that the subject will be compelled to sit through.

No Protection—security is a benefit that numerous subjects will lose until they have changed over to the new personality that is given to them. In addition to the fact that this is removed as a strategy to make the blame and misleading quality increasingly clear to the subject, however, it likewise removes the capacity the subject needs to intelligently assess the things that they are being told.

In the event that the subject is permitted to have protection, they will have room schedule-wise to secretly mull over the data they are given and may find that it is false or does not hold up to what they as of now accept. Removing this protection implies that the operator or specialists are dependably near and the subject are continually being directed to the new character.

Lack of sleep—when an individual isn't getting the measure of rest that they require they will regularly end up helpless and muddled. This can help make the perfect condition that the operator is searching for during the separating and admission phases of the indoctrinating procedure. Likewise, ordinarily, the subject will be required to do delayed physical and mental exercises over the insufficient rest so as to rush the procedure much more.

Dread—dread is an amazing inspiration and can achieve significantly more than different strategies that have been recorded. Operators may utilize dread so as to keep up the acquiescence and devotion that are wanted to the gathering. To do this, the operator may undermine the appendage, life, or soul of the subject for whatever is against the new character that is being exhibited.

These are only a couple of strategies that can be utilized during the mentally conditioning procedure. The purpose of every one of them is to impart the possibility that the old character of the subject isn't right and persuade them that the new personality is ideal.

While it is conceivable that mentally conditioning can adjust the manner in which that somebody supposes and act, most specialists accept that genuine indoctrinating is misrepresented and is impossible.

While little instances of mental programming may happen in regular day to day existence, most individuals won't find that their entire conviction frameworks have been changed through this procedure.

Chapter 11: Conspiracy Theories

We all heard about them: Loch Ness, aliens, the creepy Denver Airport, murder on J.F. Kennedy, the Illuminati, death of Queen Diana in the tunnel, or the intentional collapse of the World Trade Center plus Building 7 (which conveniently had a fire at the same time and wasn't emphasized by the news reporters at all).

The truth is, people have murdered millions of other humans in the past for power, money, or control. It wouldn't be surprising if some of these conspiracy theories proved to be true. Even though some of the ones I just mentioned are very likely to be true, and others are not, I want to mention a few that actually have turned out to be true. They were proven to be based on facts, and this shows us that we should not disregard each and each conspiracy idea just because SOME of them are ridiculous or far-fetched.

10 Federal Government Conspiracy Theories Revealed to Be True

Conspiracy theories can be interesting, outlandish and even totally looney, but are they ever true? As it turns out, they can be. Let's have a look at a handful of examples of conspiracy theories that are rooted in truth.

1. The CIA developed a heart attack gun.

As the principle goes, the CIA built a secret weapon in the '60s and '70s that could trigger fatal cardiac arrest. The weapon shot a small toxin dart that could penetrate clothing, and left absolutely nothing but a tiny red dot on the skin. The dart broke down on effect, and the target would only feel a little prick, comparable to a bug bite. Since the poison denatured quickly, it could not be spotted in an autopsy.

2. The CIA spied on, and controlled, the American media.

CIA project Operation Mockingbird spied on members of the Washington press corps in 1963, 1972 and 1973. They also paid journalists to publish CIA propaganda, wiretapped their phones and monitored their offices to keep tabs on their activities and visitors.

3. The federal government poisoned alcohol throughout Prohibition.

When the federal government banned alcohol in 1920, bootleggers would steal commercial alcohol-- used in paints, fuels, solvents and health supplies-- and redistill it for sale. Some of this alcohol included heavy metals, and caused illness or blindness. In an attempt to stop people from consuming alcohol, the federal government changed the formulas of industrial alcohol to make it entirely undrinkable. At least 10% of commercial alcohol formulas had to contain methyl alcohol, a toxin, in addition to other harmful ingredients such as kerosene, gasoline, chloroform, formaldehyde and acetone. The strategy backfired. People still drank the poisonous alcohol, and more than 10,000 people died.

4. A U.S. Air Force lab investigated the possibility of using pheromones as a weapon.

Theoretical research conducted by a United States Flying force laboratory in 1994 explored the application of a non-lethal chemical weapon called the "gay bomb." They speculated on the results of soldiers splashed in female pheromones. The goal was to make the soldiers sexually tempting to one another and adversely impact their effectiveness in battle.

5. The United States government took dead bodies for radioactive testing.

After dropping nukes on Nagasaki and Hiroshima, the U.S. federal government stole parts of dead bodies to measure the results of nuclear fallout on the human body. Scientists needed young tissue, but the agents who were recruited to find recently deceased babies and kids took samples-- including full limbs-- without the permission of the grieving families. More than 1,500 families were impacted.

6. President Woodrow Wilson's spouse ran the nation after he suffered a stroke.

After President Woodrow Wilson suffered a devastating stroke, Edith Wilson made the majority of the executive decisions in his stead. She efficiently ran the nation for well over a year, but the federal government kept it silent, for worry that it would cause a stir.

7. The CIA tested LSD and other hallucinogenic drugs on Americans.

As part of a top-secret experiment on conduct modification called MK-ULTRA, the CIA tested volunteers for a time. Ultimately, they began evaluating people without their knowledge, let alone approval, and left lots of the test subjects with irreversible psychological specials needs due to the screening.

8. The Dalai Lama was a CIA agent.

According to declassified intelligence files, in the 1960s, the CIA provided the Tibetan Resistance with $1.7 million a year to assist guerilla operations against China, including a yearly subsidy of $180,000 for the Dalai Lama.

9. The FBI spied on Beatles band member John Lennon.

A vocal supporter of the '60s and '70s anti-war counterculture, John Lennon was put under surveillance by the FBI in 1971. A year later, the Immigration and Naturalization Service attempted to deport him, but he was eventually deemed to be too affected by narcotics to act as an efficient revolutionary.

10. Canada developed a "gaydar" machine in the 1960s.

Paranoid about sexual orientation, the Canadian federal government worked with a university professor to develop a device that identified orientation in federal workers. The resulting machine gauged pupil dilation, sweating, and pulse in reaction to same-sex porn. Those tested were told that the machine's purpose was to rank their tension levels, but the truth was that the federal government wanted to remove its gay employees. Subsequently, more than 400 guys were excluded or fired from civil service, the army, and the Royal Canadian Mounted Authorities. More than 9,000 people were examined.

Chapter 12: Hypnosis- Facts, Fiction, And The Psychology That Powers It

Hypnosis is, as previously stated, the subject of much skepticism, but the modern practices of hypnotherapy and the use of altered psychological states in the interrogation of prisoners would belie the number of raised eyebrows that hypnosis receives. The theory of hypnosis actually has its origins in ancient Egypt and India, where people were encouraged to heal themselves through spiritual journeys and altered states, and through 'temple sleep', a practice which encouraged people to rest in religious places to rejuvenate their minds and bodies.

In more modern times, hypnosis has taken on several different iterations, but they are all based on the theory that the mind can be controlled through a state of trance or altered state of consciousness. We're going to pick up the history of hypnosis shortly before it became popularized by Franz Mesmer.

How Mesmer Began Mesmerizing

When Franz Mesmer was a young medical student, he studied under a Jesuit monk named Father Maximillian Hell. Hell was an astronomer and researcher who was fascinated with the natural world and with the workings of the solar system, the polar regions of the earth, and the human body. Hell developed an interest in using magnets for the power of healing and introduced his student Mesmer to the technique of magnet therapy.

Mesmer took Hell's methods of magnet therapy, which basically involved using magnetized rocks to improve the flow of fluids through the body, and adapted and expanded their uses. Mesmer would often have patients swallow iron shavings, and then use a magnet to draw those shavings through the intestinal tract. Mesmer believed that people could be cured of what ailed them should he be able to get their 'vital fluid' back on track.

Mesmer called this early technique 'animal magnetism', and he truly was convinced that he could heal people through this magnetic laying on of hands. He later developed a technique which we more closely associate with hypnosis; this method involved sitting very closely with a patient while holding their hands and occasionally rubbing their shoulders, arms, and torsos while maintaining eye contact. After a while, the patients would convulse, and all their evil or poor feelings or illness would be relieved.

Skeptical yet? So were a lot of people at the time, and in 1784 a committee was formed to investigate not Mesmer himself, but one of his proteges, a doctor named d'Eslon, who had to perform Mesmer's treatments to mixed results. Why is all this important? Because the investigating committee discovered that the treatments were complete pseudoscience and that they were rooted in 'imagination'. But they worked, sometimes, so the real question is why?

On to the Next Theory

After Mesmer's works were largely downplayed and discounted, Mesmer himself retreated from medical practice, traveling Europe and living in relative obscurity until his death in 1815. A few decades later, Scottish surgeon James Braid would be the one to finally give some credence to Mesmer's practices.

Braid was a highly acclaimed physician and surgeon who pioneered a breakthrough way to treat clubfoot and other orthopedic issues of the extremities. In 1841, Braid was invited to a healing performance by one of Mesmer's former disciples, a Frenchman named Charles Lafontaine. Lafontaine allowed doctors to come onto his stage while he was using magnetic treatments and examine his patients.

Braid was among the doctors to do so, and he observed that they all seemed to be in some sort of altered mental state. While Braid had been previously completely unconvinced that magnetism was a valid medical treatment, he was so intrigued he continued to attend Lafontaine's healing demonstrations until he could formulate a working theory as to why the treatments appeared to be successful. One thing he consistently observed was that the patients all seemed to be 'awake while sleeping'.

After some consideration, Braid concluded that the patients' altered states were a result not of Lafontaine's magnets, but of his demeanor. The magnetist's behavior is what prompted the altered state, which Braid dubbed neuro-hypnosis, from the Greek for 'nervous sleep'. Braid began experimenting with the technique at home to see if he could induce the state by himself and deduced that a hypnotic state could be produced by visual or ocular fixation. This also completely debunked the use of magnets in Lafontaine's treatments.

Braid debuted his theory of hypnotism as a psycho-physiological phenomenon late in

1841, to mixed reviews from the scientific community. In his first lecture, Braid demonstrated that he could induce the same somnolent state as Lafontaine, but without the use of magnets. Although Braid had many opponents, who refused to believe that people could be healed through the power of suggestion, he would go on to integrate hypnotism into his medical practice as an alternative or complementary treatment for the relief of pain and other physical and psychological ailments.

The Power of Belief

By now, you may have come to realize that the one component of hypnosis that we haven't discussed is the patient or subject. From the early origins of medical treatments using altered states to the modern hypnotherapies we see used today, the underlying power of these methods is that the subject must **believe** that they work. The human brain is a marvelous machine, capable of higher thought and reasoning, and responsible for making sure our heart beats and our lungs breathe.

But the brain is also a biochemical mass of electrical activity and multi-layered function. While we are usually in a state of full consciousness when we are awake, our brains are constantly working on a subconscious level, which usually manifests while we sleep. Hypnosis taps into a state of mind that is somewhere in between waking and sleeping, but it does not work if the subject does not believe that it will. We've all seen performances where audience volunteers are put into a trance and asked to complete ridiculous tasks. There are movie tropes that center on a character behaving a certain way when triggered by a hypnotic keyword. How accurate are these portrayals?

Fact and Fiction in Modern Hypnosis

Let's examine some of the present-day applications of hypnosis and see what's true and what's not. Once we've done that, you'll have a clearer picture of how hypnosis plays into psychology as a whole, and how it can be applied to dark psychology, as well.

Once Braid established a baseline for modern hypnotic techniques, it became a practice which was studied by physicians and psychologists worldwide, who wanted to figure out the biology and the psychology behind the method and determine how best to use it in their practices. Hypnosis and altered states have also been studied and adopted as techniques for military usage and prisoner interrogation, including inducing trance-like states through sleep deprivation and other methods.

In contemporary medicine, hypnosis is used for pain management and anesthetic purposes in patients who may not react well to heavy pharmaceutical treatments. It is also used as an effective complementary therapy for patients with side effects from chemotherapy, those suffering from potential rejection after organ transplant, and people with autoimmune disorders such as fibromyalgia or irritable bowel syndrome.

Modern hypnotherapy is used for a wide variety of applications, the most common being to change or break a habit, or to explore thoughts that cannot be explored in a normal state of consciousness. People use hypnotherapy to quit smoking, lose weight or stop overeating, or to aid in overcoming other addictions, like gambling.

When used to access traumatic memories or examine the underlying causes of poor behaviors, hypnotherapy must be approached with great care by a skillful practitioner. Studies have shown that mishandling hypnosis in this application can lead to false memories, distortion of perception, and implantation of the therapist's own thoughts. Here is where dark psychology can come into heavy play.

A therapist with dark intentions or anyone wishing to affect someone's brain and perceptions adversely can take a subject in a state of hypnosis and wreak psychological havoc. Therapists can willingly destroy a person's psyche by planting false memories, undermining someone's sense of self and character, and creating illusions of reality which persist once someone has roused from their hypnotic state.

It's a fact, though, that not everyone can be hypnotized, and so using hypnosis as a dark psychology technique may only be effective on a certain chunk of people. But people who are highly suggestible, who are not likely to be strong-willed enough to resist, or who are already using hypnotherapy for other applications may be the perfect subjects for dark psychological uses of hypnosis.

One of the greatest examples of this is Adolf Hitler. Hitler was a young, highly insecure World War I veteran when he was treated with hypnotherapy for hysterical blindness stemming from post-traumatic stress from combat. While in an altered state, Hitler's therapist told him that only he could cure his own blindness and that he was very special and destined for great things. Hitler's therapist unwittingly conditioned him to believe that he was going to be a ruler of men and save the world from unseen evils, while in reality, he himself had become the evil.

Stage hypnotists, like we see in dinner theater, are not practicing safe hypnosis, either. Although these shows are meant to be funny, these entertainers are tapping into one of the darker sides of the hypnotic effect--the ability to induce hallucinations and psychosis. Hallucinations are the perception that something is there that is not; commonly this manifests as seeing or hearing things that are not present. Psychosis is a full-blown altered mental state, which causes people to act in a manner completely out of character for their regular behavior or personality.

A common theme of hypnosis stage shows is having people cluck like a chicken.

Hypnosis is not something to be taken lightly. It can have lasting psychological impacts on those it is practiced on. Whether those impacts are good or bad is completely dependent on the skill and the intent of the hypnotist. If you wished to learn hypnosis as a skill for implementing dark psychology, you'd have a serious weapon in your mental arsenal. It's practicality, however, is something to be considered. Because many people are not susceptible to hypnotic suggestion, its use in dark psychology has limited real-life applications.

Chapter 13: How Dark Psychology Is Used In Relationships

Both men and women to get what they want use dark psychology in relationships all the time. So In this section, we will talk about how both men and women make use of dark psychology to manipulate and influence the opposite sex.

Dark Methods that women use to manipulate men

Safety, Significance and worthwhile

They do it through safety significance and worthwhile. The first thing that they do is to make you feel safe because when you are out in the cold and your boss yells at you, and you get offended, and you are on the way home, and the traffic was awful, you know that somebody is there waiting for you to comfort you. So women may make you feel safe and secure, and you may feel like, "isn't it nice to have a woman that will take care of you." so that is one thing they do.

They make you feel significant

Now then the second thing that they do is to make you feel significant, and they do that by saying, "I love you. I need you, and I believe in you, you are everything to me. How I never do anything to hurt you. I am your best friend, and you are my best friend. And you can count on me for anything. I got you at your back'. So they make you feel significant.

Make you feel like the king of the Castle

The next thing is that they make you feel like the king of the castle, and you're worthwhile. They become your number one cheerleader. They tell you that you can do anything and you can get a new promotion and when you feel so great about yourself, you will like to be with them. So they really use loving words. These are all elements of true love because true love makes you feel safe, makes you feel significant, and makes you feel worthwhile, but then when the true love is being used in a wrong way to take advantage of somebody, that is manipulation. And they also try to make you feel worthwhile and then they make you feel cocky and hot. And once you get hot, it's hard to walk away, and that is when the safety, significance, and feeling worthwhile really kicks in.

Dark methods that men use to manipulate women

This session will show you how you can go out on a date to meet new guys. You probably have a self-help book, but for some reason, you get stuck up, tripped up, used abused and left broken-hearted, and trying to pick up the pieces of what you did for the last 2 to 3 years. In this section, we will talk about the method that guys use to manipulate even the smartest girls.

The method of Mirroring

And that method is called the method of mirroring. This is the principle that most men use to manage and get into your heart, your bed, and your life. The first of all, seek you out. Men are hunters, and you are their prey. So someone that looks cool approaches you sits down and asks you some questions, and you are taking back by their romantic gestures. They buy you a drink, and they take you dancing, or maybe even deliver some flowers to your home or to your office. And before you know it, you are now telling them everything about yourself. You are now telling them that you like dogs or that you are allergic to cats, and you like kids and your career goals.

You also tell them your religious views and whether you do yoga or whether you meditate, or whether you are into yoga and what your astrological sign is. And everything else from the top of your head to the tip of your toes. But what you don't realize is that everything that they have done is to give them the way to manipulate you and guide you into their arms, and it is called the mirroring principle.

They're going to use every freaking thing that you have spilled out against you. They will tell you that since you like dogs, then they like dogs. They will tell you that since you like football, they like football too. They will tell you that since you love cats, then they Love cats too. If you tell them that you love to go to the ballet, they will tell you that they like to go to ballet too, but then you will realize 20 years after you are married to them, that you have never been to a ballet. But what you don't realize is that you were a victim of mirroring. The BS they tell you to win you over, works. But then something else happens, and when you wake up with the person, and then you realize that you are stuck with them just like the way they are stuck with you.

They don't like to go to Ballet, they hate New York, and they can't stand how much money you spend on clothes. They will never figure out why you think family is so important. Even though you have adamantly expressed that to them in the first year that you guys were together. But then you get into a freaking mess you get into a relationship with a stranger because he is using the mirroring technique against you. Now the mirroring technique is very good in a job position, but it is not good for you to use it. It is good to narrow their body language in a job interview.

Shut your mouth

Now what you should do when someone is using his technique against you is not act fake or lie but to be smart. You like the guy, but when he approaches, you shut your mouth up. When you're trying to pick a lifetime mate, the two most important question that you are ever going to ask yourself is where you are going and who you are taking with you. So if you have spilled out all your personal information and they are marrying you because you are absolutely fabulous, then you're not going to get the real deal. So what you should do is to pull back and put on any emotional Mask and let them talk.

And eventually, they are going to spill their guts to you. They will tell you that their life is kind of chaotic that they want to have a good time and they don't really know what they want, and their life is kind of chaotic, but most times you won't listen to that because you are too busy selling yourself. Because of your low self-esteem, you are trying to tell them how wonderful you are and how low cut your dress is and how much education you have, and then they drop you because you aren't listening.

So put some kind of neuron and pull back a little bit. Follow your heart. Follow your attraction, but use your head. Let them feed you with all their life happenings. And if you let them sit there long enough and smile sweetly at them and don't interject your thoughts to them, then they will tell you the truth. So, therefore, you can then go home and either pencil them into your black book or put him into your cellphone, look him up on Facebook or keep moving.

Because you don't have time to waste on a Crip or on someone who is using the mirror of your true self, your loving self, your adorable self to be manipulated and lied to. You should look in the mirror and see all the great qualities that you have. You don't have to oversell yourself. You don't have to manipulate him into bed or keep him interested. You don't have to ask him to marry you. It is all B.S. it is all crap. Because you are not your true self and your true self is just what everybody wants. Always remember that you should follow your heart as long as it is not above your head. You remember not to get manipulated by men.

Subliminal messaging

Now let us talk about subliminal messaging; now these are messages that are designed to go on detected by your unconscious mind and to be understood by your conscious mind. Now, this sounds sneaky because it is sneaky. So many companies have been doing this over the years all the way from soda companies showing sexy ladies on the bottles and making you feel like if you drink that soda, it makes you sexy or to make you feel healthier, happier, and have a healthier relationship.

Companies do use many sexual references, whether it is the way that the bubbles arise through so that when somebody drinks, it just to get you to think about sex because sex sells. There have been several research behind the music of the commercial, and the research shows that using words like hungry or buy is very powerful. And these words pass our conscious mind, and it's heard by our unconscious mind. We can be influenced, and that is why we need to stay mindful of the people that we are following by knowing why we are following them.

If following someone only makes you feel like you need to buy more things, then maybe it is time for us to unfollow them because after knowing about how businesses get you to spend more money on their product, you shouldn't underestimate the power of marketing and psychological research. Because they are utilizing all those tools to make you make a purchase, and we are being marketed to all the time from both TV and social media. There are advertisements everywhere, so you should try to be cognitive about what you are buying and why you buy it.

Ask yourself, is it because you feel influenced by what somebody said or did, or is it because you actually need to buy that item or is it something that you have been saving up for, and you want to buy it. So there are certain things that you should put in place so that you will be mindful of what you buy and why you are buying it.

Chapter 14: Factors That Make You Vulnerable To Manipulation

Everyone has a gut instinct that rears up when they are used or misguided. Your gut instinct is very sound. You will know when you are a victim. The problem is, a lot of people ignore their instincts. You might ignore yours. You might think something like, "I'm just paranoid" or "What could go wrong if I hang out with this person?" You might think that the harm will be worth the benefits that you could get from knowing this person who gives you bad vibes. Maybe everyone else likes this guy, do you think that you are just weird, and you should like him too. Or maybe he is able to charm you and convince you that he is not so bad, and over time you start to get over your initial bad vibes.

But vibes are not something that you should ever ignore. The minute your gut warns you about someone, listen. Your first impression of someone is never wrong. If you get a terrible first impression, don't give the person a second chance. You know more about someone by just glancing at them than you would think. The human brain is amazingly powerful; you only are conscious of roughly ten percent of your mind, so a lot is going on under the surface that you are not consciously aware of. Your brain is capable of reading people and determining the future far more than you realize.

So, when you get that gut feeling, understand that your brain is working very hard and noticing things that you are not consciously aware of. The person that you get bad vibes may not be matching his body language to his words, or he may be acting oddly in ways that you can't detect easily. Listen to your gut!

If you are just not in touch with your gut at all, or if you have doubts about someone, you might want to consider looking at some other signs. You can identify a manipulator based on his actions and language choices. You can also tell by how you feel around this person. Various clues point out who someone is and what his intentions are.

What Makes You Vulnerable

You may wonder why manipulators are attracted to you, especially if you have had multiple encounters with manipulative types. You may also wonder what you should change about yourself to avoid running into a manipulator in the future.

One thing that makes you vulnerable is being accepted to manipulative treatment and emotional abuse. If you were emotionally abused or repressed as a child, this type of treatment might seem normal to you. You don't know anything else. You don't know how a healthy relationship is supposed to feel. So, you accept the terrible treatment that others would not think of accepting. As a result, you are projecting a sense of vulnerability that draws manipulators from far away. The minute you begin to tolerate their treatment and keep them in your life, they gain power over you and choose to continue using you until they get what they want. Work on increasing your self-esteem and avoiding familiar patterns. If you get that eerie sense of déjà vu when you meet someone, you might want to avoid that person because he is probably reminding you of abusive patterns that you have been in.

Another thing that may make you vulnerable is neediness or weakness. If you are in a vulnerable time in life, you might be more open to manipulators. Manipulators can see that you are in need, and they see it as an opportunity to offer you what you need in exchange for what they want. They will use any opportunity to gain control over you, and when you are in a bad period of life, you hand them opportunities. You need to guard your heart and mind, especially well when you are at a disadvantage. Be wary of extremely kind strangers or lifesavers. Not all heroes are good guys. Your heroes may help you, but they may have hidden intentions. Most people won't do something for free, so watch out.

You may also be a target for manipulation if you have low self-esteem. Events in your life or your childhood may have stripped away from your self-esteem and confidence. You may be emotionally vulnerable. So, you want people who build up your ego. Manipulators can spot this, and they will move in on you, working hard to please you and make you smile. They see a way into your mind through your bruised ego. Try to build your self-esteem by yourself and work on loving yourself.

Signs of a Manipulator

A manipulator is often incredibly superficial. This means that he looks good on the outside, but there is nothing to follow it up on the inside. He is shallow and lacks depth. Everything he does and says is fake, part of a façade that he erects to fool you. So, beware of people who are incredibly charming and attractive when you first meet them. Get to know them before you start confiding in them or trusting them. Don't make a commitment or business deal until you are sure of yourself.

Another sign of a manipulator is that you feel compelled to confide in him or to do what he wants. You always find yourself saying yes when you want to say no. It's impossible to be yourself and to stand up for yourself. He has some sort of power over you that you can't resist. Unfortunately, this power is just a carefully woven web of manipulation, deception, and emotional harm. He will dump you the minute he gets all that he can from you, so don't stick around or make the mistake of thinking that this relationship will last. He does not care, no matter how well he pretends to. Get away from him before the relationship gets too harmful, and he ruins your life.

You may also find yourself saying sorry all of the time. Your guilt eats you up. Every situation with this person seems like your fault. Even if he is at fault, he manages to twist things around so that you feel guilty. He will never take responsibility for anything that he does, and he will always put everything on you. He can do what he wants, but he holds you to exacting standards and punishes you when you don't follow suit. He kills your self-esteem and causes you to hate yourself.

Finally, a manipulator is great at changing your mind. You might feel one way, but after talking with him, you feel a completely different way. He can change your mind and your way of thinking. Sometimes this may even be a good thing, as he makes you think more constructively or positively. But be wary of someone who has so much power over your moods and your thoughts.

Chapter 15: Hostile Mind Takeover

Brainwashing. A pretty scary word, right?

Thankfully, it's not a thing most of us have to worry about. True brainwashing takes time and the subject has to be kept in a situation that breaks them in ways one can't be broken unless held captive.

Wikipedia defines this best - Mind control is also known as **brainwashing**, coercive persuasion, mind abuse, thought control, or thought reform and all these words refer to a process in which a group or individual systematically uses unethically manipulative methods to persuade others to conform to the wishes of the manipulator, often to the detriment of the person being manipulated.

So let's see what all is involved in this lengthy process, shall we?

Repetition

You did it. You did it. You did it. If you're seated in a small room you are locked in and cannot leave, escape by falling asleep, or ignore the person saying this over and over, the chances are that you will finally admit to something even if you didn't do it.

If it will shut the person up, you would agree to anything.

Annoying someone often gets them what they wanted.

Being annoying might seem like it shouldn't work. And it won't if the other person can get away from the annoying person. But we can't always get away from people who are making us crazy by asking things or saying things over and over again.

Even something that is making the same noise over and over or continuously will have you changing your mind, no matter how well it was made up, just to shut them up.

Think about your baby who is crying in their crib because they don't want to go to sleep alone. They've been fed, bathed, burped, put a dry diaper on and everything should be fine for them just to drink their bottle and go night-night.

Only you loved them so much when they were first born that you just couldn't stand to lay them down after they fell to sleep in your arms. No, you held them and rocked them as you gazed down at their darling little sleeping face.

But then the months passed, and the baby got bigger and you felt like the time had come to let them learn how to go to sleep on their own. But that baby doesn't want to do that. And that baby has a lung capacity to rival the best swimmers on the planet. And it will continue to cry, scream, and throw everything it can until you give in.

And you will give in. We all do. The sound can drive a person crazy and you can't walk away and leave your baby all alone so you can get away from the sound.

Bad people took this innate nature of people and learned how to use it against them. They learned that if you removed the person's capability to leave your presence, then you could effectively pound what you want into their heads.

Most people don't have any good intentions when they set out to do this. And what you really need to watch out for are the authorities. They take you to a small room – the interrogation room. This is a room that you aren't supposed to get up and walk out of. They have you trapped and sometimes they do lock the door to make sure you don't leave.

What you need to know – Do not talk without having a lawyer present!!!

No matter what they say or do or try to get you to say or do, don't do a thing except say that you need to get a lawyer before you say a word.

First – they have already taken away your ability to leave their presence. This gives them the time to keep repeating things to you and manipulating your mind. And we all now know that most of us can be made to think things that aren't true. Our minds are more susceptible than any of us really knew!

Imitation

When we imitate someone's body language and some of the words they use often, we make them think we are like-minded. People like it when others believe the way they do, like the things they do and have the same types of goals that they do.

You have to make the person think you have their best interest at heart if you are to truly brainwash them.

Saying Don't Instead Of Can't

You can trick your mind into thinking that you came up with the idea that you don't want to do something rather than that you can't.

Why?

We hate to be told what to do as children and adults. It's just part of being human.

If you are on a strict diet and someone asks if you'd like a donut, you might say that you can't have one because you're on a diet. But that might make your brain spark up and it will tell you that you can't be told what to do by anyone.

So, you trick your mind. If asked if you want a donut, you can say, "No, I don't want one. Thanks though." That way it won't wake up that part of your brain that thinks it shouldn't be told why it can and can't do.

Rituals

Rituals help us to accept things. Back in your school days, you most likely had a morning ritual that helped you get to school. Without a ritual, you would most likely miss a lot of school as you might just wake up and think you would rather not go that day and roll over and go back to sleep.

So, your parents instilled a ritual to help you get up and get to school. The alarm goes off in your parents' room and you begin to stir as you hear it. Your mother comes to the side of your bed, kissing your cheek. "Time to wake up for school, honey. I'll get breakfast going while you hop in the shower, then brush your teeth and hair, then get dressed and come to the breakfast table."

So, you rolled out of bed, groaning and maybe even complaining a little, "Aw, Mom, I don't want to go to school today. Can't I just stay sleeping?"

"Don't be silly. Now off to the shower, young man."

After a shower, you feel more awake and as each ritual is completed you wake up a bit more and now you're on the routine, moving right along as you do each day.

And this routine sets you up for having a job one day where you will develop something similar to get you into the right mind frame to do whatever it is you need to do.

Saying Excited Instead Of Afraid

Another brain trick is using excited instead of afraid. Rollercoasters can be used for this example. You're standing in the long line for hours and your mind can really mess with you in that amount of time.

You start to shake as you hear the screams coming from the ride you're about to get on. "I better not go."

Others around you, coax you to stay. "Come on. It's exciting!"

You start to think in that way and get okay with taking the ride. "Okay, you're right."

But you will flip flop between being afraid and being excited. And the thing is that you actually experience the same exact physical things with both emotions.

Only your brain sees one as positive – excitement. And it sees the other – fear – as negative. So, one is great as the other is unacceptable.

Putting Reasoning Behind A Request

You've got a big favor to ask someone that you know won't want to do it.

What do you do?

You put a great reason why you need this done immediately behind your request.

"Can you clean out the gutters, honey?" You don't wait more than a beat to go on, "Because if it rains, and rain is in today's forecast, the water won't flow through the gutters and take it away from the house instead, it'll pool on the roof and we'll get leaks. We don't want that."

Most people will do things if they know there's a reason why it needs to be done.

All Choices Lead To The Same Conclusion

In my opinion, this is the laziest of all the mind manipulation tricks. First of all, it shows no real insight into the human mind. Thinking that anyone, other than a very little kid, would truly believe that they only have three choices about anything is rather silly.

Let's say that you only have vanilla ice cream in the freezer and that's what you want your kid to pick. "So, you can have some apples for dessert. Or you can have some prunes. Or you can have vanilla ice cream."

What is any kid going to pick? Ice cream.

In the adult version of this, you might have a husband and wife who are house hunting. Tired of looking at every house on the market, the husband narrows it down to three houses. "You can pick the yellow one with the shady yard. You can pick the brown one with the big dining room. Or you can pick the blue one with the wrap around porch."

"Only those three? Why only them?" she'd ask. "There are fifty other ones to pick from. You're crazy if you think I'm going to just pick out of those."

The thing about all the house he gave her to pick from was that all of those had what he wanted in a home — a two-car garage. But she shot him down.

Maybe if he'd just been honest about wanting a two-car garage in the first place, his wife might've made that a priority to her as well.

Giving people the chance to work with you is a lot better than trying to trick them into getting them to do what you want.

Assault On One's Identity

This is when someone attempts to tell you that you are not who you think you are. You are not a woman. You are not a wife. You are not someone's child. You are not anyone. You are not anything. You're void.

It might seem like something that no one would fall for, but if these mantras are repeated over and over again for extended periods of time, then most people do begin to believe that about themselves — they are no one.

Key Takeaways

Using repetition will get you the results you are looking for.

Imitating someone will make them feel more comfortable with you and more susceptible to your mental manipulations.

Using don't in the place of can't make it seem like you have made the decision not to do something, instead of it not being allowed.

Rituals help to cement things into your brain.

Using excited instead of afraid can be a good way to trick your mind into experiencing negative things in a positive way.

When you make a request, putting the reasoning behind that makes it more likely to be accepted.

When offering choices when you are trying to manipulate them, you will want all the choices to come to the same conclusions.

By assaulting someone's identity, you can break them down to nothing so that you can build them back up into the person you want them to be.

Exercises

You really want a house with a swimming pool, but you think your spouse won't want that. What technique would you use to get what you want and why?

If an officer of the law asks you to come down to the station to talk to them about a crime, what will you do about that?

If someone tells you that you are not who you think you are, how will you deal with that?

If you want someone to accept the things they must do, what would you implement to help them accept the fact?

Conclusion

There are many people out there with big goals and dreams of their own, who will let these go by the wayside because they are too worried about what others will think about them, about how this is going to go against the ethical and moral codes that they have, and about who is going to get hurt in the process.

If this all sounds like something you would be worried about, this guidebook was probably not the right choice for you to look through. We spent a lot of time taking a look at dark psychology and the different shady tactics that you can use to get what you want out of life. From persuasion to manipulation to your unique skills and characteristics as an empath, you will learn throughout this guidebook the exact steps you need to use to use the different methods and techniques of dark psychology and get the results you need.

When you are ready to get what you want out of life finally, and you are tired of waiting for others to hand it to you. You are tired of being kind and finding that life is passing you by with no benefits, promotions, or anything else that you need to reach your goals, then make sure to check out this guidebook and learn how to make dark psychology work for your needs!

www.ingramcontent.com/pod-product-compliance
Lightning Source LLC
Chambersburg PA
CBHW071432070526
44578CB00001B/78